- LARGE PRINT -

Small Blessings

Celestine Sibley

G.K.HALL &CO.

 Boston, Massachusetts

1978

Library of Congress Cataloging in Publication Data

Sibley, Celestine.
  Small blessings.

  Large print ed.
  1. Meditations. 2. Large type books. I. Title.
[BV4832.2.S5233 1978] 242'.4 78-56
ISBN 0-8161-6570-X

Grateful acknowledgment is made to the following for permission to reprint previously published material:

David McKay Company, Inc.: Excerpts from "The Snail" in *Stalking the Far-away Places* by Euell Gibbons. Copyright © 1973 by Euell Gibbons. "To a Friend" from *Stalking the Good Life* by Euell Gibbons. Copyright © 1971 by Euell Gibbons.

Random House, Inc.: Excerpt from "How Flowers Changed the World" from *The Immense Journey* by Loren Eiseley. Copyright © 1957 by Loren Eiseley. Excerpt from *Louisville Saturday* by Margaret Long. Copyright 1950 by Margaret Long.

Published in Large Print by arrangement with Doubleday & Company, Inc.

Set in Compugraphic 18 pt English Times

Contents

Small Blessings

A few years ago when many counties still had what they frankly and unabashedly called "almshouses," instead of places now euphemistically known as Happy Hearts Haven and Sunset Manor, I became friends with an old man who may have been the richest person ever to inhabit a poorhouse.

He had absolutely no possessions, except the rusty old suit, the grayish food, and the grayish dormitory bed the county gave him, and yet he glowed with happiness. He wasn't as you might suppose, a mental case, unaware of his surroundings and his situation in life. On the contrary, he was the *most aware* person I ever saw.

1

In his younger days he had been a successful lawyer, but his wife had died, he took to drink, and a series of miserable circumstances had resulted in his being disbarred. He lost his profession and his home, he had no money, and by the time a county welfare worker found him he was weakened by starvation and near death from pneumonia. Although he was seventy years old and apparently had no reason to make the effort to live, he rallied and recovered.

When I knew him he was a jaunty little fellow who walked miles in the nearby park every day, spent hours watching birds, and had not missed a sunrise for ten years.

I used to visit him for sheer pleasure in his company and the luxury of being cheered up when things were not going well with me. He never failed me. He had the florid speech of one who in his youth had been nurtured on the classics, and sometimes when we sat on a bench under a tree he would pull his stately courtroom manner on me.

"If it please your Honor," he would

sometimes begin, and he often prefaced a statement with "I submit to you." Sometimes he left me puzzled and unsure of his exact meaning, but I usually had a feeling about what he was telling me and frequently it would come clear later.

There was the day he interrupted a story he was telling me about some intramural skirmish among the inmates of the almshouse to stare out across the field and cry, "To know . . . to *know!* That is the sum total of discovery! Read your Plato, madam."

Being abysmally literal-minded I asked, "What? To know what?"

"The subject of knowledge," he said impatiently, "is to know — to *know.* To see, to feel, to understand, to *know!*"

Another day he came down the almshouse steps to greet me, swinging his cane as if he didn't need it to lean on. When he reached me he searched my face intently and said, "Are you happy?"

"We-ell," I began, playing for time.

He stalked ahead of me to the bench under the tree. "Sit down," he directed, "and think. What do you have to be happy about?''

For some time I had been thinking what I had to be *unhappy* about and I was not so facile with the exercise in reverse. But quickly I went over in my mind the things that I automatically considered sources of happiness, although at times they were a plague and a pestilence — my children, if only they would behave themselves, my parents, our old house, which nagged me with its need for paint and repairs, my job.

When I had enumerated them to myself I started to tick them off to him.

''Never mind!'' he said impatiently. ''I don't need to know. *''You* need to know.''

And then he told me why. The greatest waste in life, he said, is not to know when you are happy, not to store up good fortune and rejoice in it when you have it but to wait until the end of life and look back in surprise and say, ''I was happy then. Why didn't I know it? If only . . . . ''

''Know!'' he directed. *''Know!* Otherwise it is all a waste.''

Presently we talked of other things, and when I left he was checking a crape myrtle tree at the edge of the yard to measure the progress of a couple of nest-building brown thrashers.

A week later he died while taking one of his long walks through the park. He had insisted on going out in the midst of a thunderstorm, although the superintendent had tried to keep him in. I couldn't feel sorry for that, even as the aggrieved superintendent told me about it, because it did seem to me that in his way he had taken friend Plato's advice. He had emulated the swans, which have sung all their lives, when they come to die "do then sing more lustily than ever." His daily walk was his own special kind of singing.

In the years since that day under the tree at the almshouse, the last time I saw my old friend, I have thought often of his advice. An awareness of the *nowness* of happiness is not easy come by. It takes practice. When my children were small they called it listing their "thankfuls." There are plenty of troubles in life and I am not sure what to do about them, but I think one way of keeping them in perspective is to know when we hold happiness in our hands and to get the maximum pleasure and satisfaction out of that. There will be times when, as the old hymn has it, "life's dark maze I tread and griefs around me spread." Unfortunately, it doesn't take much practice to feel pain. But you have to look sharp, you have to pay attention, to catch small, quiet, often fleeting blessings and know them for what they are.

So this book is really a kind of memo to myself, a reminder of the minor — or maybe they are major — goodnesses in life. And I would be immeasurably enriched if it should serve to steer one other person toward what my old friend in the almshouse practiced daily, an exercise in awareness.

Apple Trees

Sometimes I feel sorry for people who don't have an apple tree.

Where I grew up there were grapefruit and pomegranate and fig trees. Everybody had an abundance of bananas from the fruit wharf, and although the climate was not ideal for their culture, we also grew peaches. But apples were not an everyday supermarket staple then. We always had them at Christmas, and usually in the fall my father's cousin in West Virginia would send us a barrel of winesaps, which lasted most of the winter. They were as special as they were beautiful and I grew up regarding apple trees as storybook trees.

Starting with the Bible and the Fall and going on through Greek and Roman mythology to northern-locale children's stories, there were always apple trees. Jo March hid out in an apple tree to read. The Greek princess Atlanta was so attracted by apples that she stopped to pick them up when losing her race with Hippomenes meant losing her life. One of my favorite fairy stories revealed to me that when you slice across an apple you will always find a star at its heart — due to an act of kindness the apple tree performed at some time in its history.

The apple was a symbol of love and beauty to the Greeks and Romans and a symbol of faraway northern climes and storybook children to me.

It was not only a beautiful fruit but one that you could eat without doing anything to it except maybe polishing it on your sleeve or the hem of your skirt, making it the ideal accompaniment for reading by the fire or hiking in the woods. With Francie in *A Tree Grows in Brooklyn,* who always felt a sense of comfort in knowing that there was a pot of coffee on the stove and you could drink it if you wanted to, I always felt secure that there was something good to eat in the house if we had apples.

The first time I saw apples actually growing on trees I was so moved I wept and nearly missed the bus on my maiden voyage to New York City. Four friends and I were taking advantage of the Greyhound one-hundred-dollar round-trip excursion rate from Mobile to Manhattan. We had spent one night in Montgomery, due to engine trouble on the way, and at the end of the second day out had progressed only as far as Cornelia, a little town in the north Georgia mountains. It was about twilight when the bus approached Cornelia, and although we were vigorous teen-agers, we were stiff with weariness and had that crusted feeling that you get from sleeping on a bus with your mouth open and dust flying in through the window.

The others were already tired of the expedition and half blaming me because I had been the prime promoter of it. I had even begun to question the charms of travel a little myself when my eye fell on something red gleaming among the leaves of a tree by the roadside.

"Apples?" I whispered and then yelled, *"Apples!"*

The bus driver confirmed it. We were in apple-orchard country. There was even a monument to the apple in the little town we were approaching.

My friends hooted but I couldn't help it, I was all choked up. I hung my head out the bus window and looked and looked at the beautiful red fruit hanging like Christmas tree ornaments from the green trees. When the bus stopped I was out the door in a flash and on the ground running toward the nearest apple tree. I got my hand on the cool satiny skin of a live, growing apple and, of course, intended to pick it, but there was something about the moment, something so moving, I couldn't bring myself to steal it. I knew from my reading that stealing apples was an acceptable crime in cold climes like that of stealing watermelons in a warm clime. But I couldn't do it. I just stood there and looked up into the branches of that apple tree, breathed in the winy fragrance of its fruit, and cried.

Naturally I had to have apples and there were some for sale there by the bus stop. So I bought a sackful, and then I strolled across the street to see the big red apple monument.

It was then the bus left me.

My friends, tired and dozing, didn't miss me for some time, and when they did they had a hard time persuading the bus driver to turn around and go back for me. Far from being frightened at being left in a strange town without money or a suitcase, I had some idiot notion that the world was well lost for apples. When the bus finally returned and I reboarded it I blissfully passed my sack full of apples up and down the aisle with the pride of one offering rubies.

"She's a fool for apples, ain't she?" the bus driver asked.

If that statement was right then — and I'd have been the last to deny it — it's practically oracular now. Twelve years ago I lucked into a little log cabin in a community named, of all things, Sweet

Apple. (There's another, bigger and more suburban settlement five miles away called Crabapple.) Sweet Apple got its name from a row of old sweet apple trees which had stood in that cabin's yard many years ago. Only their carcasses were left by the time I found and bought the deserted little place, but there was one in the backyard still in comparative health and still bearing. It's a seedling, I am sure, but its presence there fills me with delight.

It has green June apples on it which are tart to eat raw but make wonderful pies. Neighbors who have known the old tree longer than I have often come with baskets and buckets to get a few apples for pies and turnovers.

When it is not bearing, the tree seems equally lovely to me. It is old and gnarled with a lichened gray trunk well perforated by woodpeckers, for, of course, it never knew spray or even pruning before I came and it has seldom known it since. Once when we first found Sweet Apple cabin I thought the old apple tree needed pruning, and our neighbor, Mr. Lum Crow, offered to undertake the job. I think often of seeing him, a seventy-nine-year-old gentleman, sitting like God in Thornton Wilder's *Our Town* in the top of the tree, carefully trimming off the dead branches and talking serenely of life and weather and plowing.

In spite of its age and generally neglected scraggliness, my apple tree looks opulent and fulfilled when it is bearing and bone spare and graceful when it is dormant. And in between there is that magical period when its old gray branches somehow open up to release a delicate pale pink froth of fragrant blossoms and soft gray-green leaves.

Sometimes it seems to me that apple trees are a joy all their lives, for, of course, when you plant them there's the excitement of watching them grow. In the spring they bloom, in June they bear, the rest of the summer they offer shade for our lawn chairs, in fall and winter they are driftwood beautiful, and when they come to die and have to be cut down their logs make a blaze in the fireplace a poem of color and fragrance.

Peter Wynne, a writer with a fine

affection for the apple, in a beautiful book called *Apples — History, Folklore, Horticulture and Gastronomy* told how Plutarch and some of his pals held a symposium on the subject of why the apple tree is called "the bearer of splendid fruit." They decided that "the best qualities in all fruits were combined in the apple," that it was smooth to the touch, imparted a sweet odor to the hand without soiling it, and was sweet to the taste and pleasing to the eyes and nose.

Sometimes I go out and sit under my apple tree and feel sorry for people who don't have one.

Neighbors

Once I heard of a woman who lived in an apartment in Chicago for ten years without knowing her neighbors on either side, upstairs or down. I didn't believe it when I heard it and I still don't. To me living in a world without neighbors would be tantamount to choosing to dwell forever in solitary confinement. Neighbors are the greatest convenience since indoor plumbing — a source of help, safety, comfort, and fun. They share your grief and, best of all, your joy. For didn't somebody wise once say that we can bear grief alone but not joy?

We cherished our neighbors in town, although we were so close to one another we inevitably raised the city dweller's classic barriers to preserve privacy. We weren't in and out of one another's houses at whim, but we spoke when we met, called out from front porches or over back hedges, helped in small, cup-of-sugar ways, and when trouble struck we rallied round. Our neighbors bought tickets to the school carnival reliably every fall and Girl Scout cookies by the gross. They lent rakes and hoes and were patient about broken windows in baseball season and trombone and piano practice through music-lesson years. They picked up the mail and the newspaper when we were out of town, forgave our dog when he buried bones in their flower beds, brought covered dishes when we had a death in the family.

Once when Mary disappeared from a playmate's sandbox about suppertime and was missing for four or five hours, neighbors were at my house before the police were, putting on the coffeepot, answering the phone, standing by. They even advised against spanking when Mary was brought home about midnight, howling with indignation because we had

16

three police cars in front of our house and she had missed all the excitement. (She had been visiting another neighbor we didn't even know.)

Oh, I loved and valued my city neighbors, and when I moved to the country, where next-door is out of sight and the nearest loaf of bread three miles away, I feared that I would have to learn to live without neighbors at all. It was nonsense. Neighboring in the country, because of distances, isolation, and long stretches of loneliness in the old pretelephone, pretelevision days, is an art, an essential art. The old traditions of logrollings and barn-raisings, of quilting bees and dinners on the ground, still prevail in Sweet Apple settlement despite the encroachments of suburbia. We may not have an ox to get out of the ditch these days, but if we have a problem of any kind it gets top priority with our neighbors.

One of the first people to shoulder our crises as if they were his own was W. H. Smellie, called "Doc" by one and all. An urbane gentleman who moved to the country late in life, Doc was a quick study. Now in his seventies, he is the neighborhood's number-one troubleshooter, his energy and strength matching his wit and good humor.

One night the first winter I was at Sweet Apple I arrived home late, bringing with me my grandson Bird, who was then but one year old. We heard water running as we got out of the car and walked toward the cabin, and I hurried in to find a pipe in the bathroom had slipped its moorings and was pouring a Mississippi flood over the cabin walls and floors. I had a sleepy, bewildered baby on my hands, a cold house, and water everywhere. On top of that, the phone started ringing. Somehow I sloshed to it. It was Doc.

"Everything all right down there?" he boomed cheerfully.

"No, Doc!" I wailed. "We're under water. A pipe's doing funny!"

"Funny, is it?" Doc said, laughing. Then he quickly determined how "funny," instructed me in turning off the water at the well, and said he would be right over.

Within moments Doc's car was in the driveway and he was clanking in with a handful of tools.

Another winter morning I awakened to find my pipes frozen and not a drop of water in the house. In a little while Doc pulled up. He was making rounds, checking the situation of the mechanically helpless. He had a few plastic jugs of water, which his wife, Verda, keeps for emergencies, and a blow torch. Right away he lit up his torch and crawled under the cabin to thaw the ice-clogged pipes.

I hovered at the corner of the house, shivering in the cold north wind but ready to hand him tools.

"Go in there and call Verda for me," Doc said to get me in the house out of the wind. "Tell her I'm over here warming up a frigid widow."

To Verda's credit when I repeated the message to her verbatim, she laughed. She runs a relatively trouble-free household herself, making it possible for Doc to help out the neighbors in time of stress. If the well breaks down or the lawnmower stops or you have unexpected company and nothing to eat in the house, Doc arrives with tools, know-how, and steaks. If you plan a party and forget ice or charcoal, Doc and Verda are better than the 7-11 and a lot closer. I have run out of gas miles from home and called Doc because I knew he would bring it cheerfully and not lecture me for my carelessness as he did.

We had a brutally sick old dog that we were going to have to put out of her misery. Doc lent us his pistol and then, seeing that we weren't going to have the guts for this act of mercy, he drove us into the house, led the old dog to the woods, and shot her himself — with tears in his eyes.

When a guest of honor for a party we were planning showed up a day early and I didn't know what to do with him while we cut the grass and polished the silver, Doc was there. He took the visitor sight-seeing and to lunch, getting him back just as the fiddles were tuning up for the square dance. Then Doc stayed to call the sets for the dance and lead the singing when the party progressed to that.

It might be possible to live in the country without Doc and Verda, but I don't think we would like it, any more than we have adjusted to the loss of Olivia Johnson and her brother-in-law Quinton Johnson. The Johnson family — the three brothers, Quinton, Clarence, and Paul, and their wives and children and grandchildren — have been our closest neighbors, helpful in time of need but, better than that, available for fun, good stories, reminiscence, country lore.

The death of Quinton a few years ago was a loss from which Sweet Apple settlement may never recover. He was a plain man, scantily educated but with a wisdom and patience a sage would envy. I can still see him, as we saw him so often, a slow-moving, quiet-voiced, overalled figure, plodding down the road with a fishing pole over his shoulder and a swirl of hound puppies around his feet.

Or sometimes he rattled up in his old blue pickup truck and lifted his carpenter's tools out of the back, ready to hang a door or build a shed or do some odd job that could involve laying a rock wall or digging up a septic tank or coping with a rebellious water heater.

A member of that big family who came down from the mountains and scrabbled out a precarious living during the hard days of the Depression, Quinton was a resourceful man. His big hands, his strong sinewy arms could take on any task, and more than once he explained to me that willingness was often what he had instead of skill.

We met him when we were shoring up Sweet Apple cabin. He came one sleety winter day when we were trying to put a big beam back in place after replacing some of the rotten logs with sound ones from the back of the house. We didn't know what we were doing ourselves, and Quinton, smiling kindly at our efforts, did what he called with poetic simplicity "taking aholt." I'll never forget sitting there in the empty, half-put-together little house and watching the sure, strong blows of his hammer on the spike-sized nails as he sent them straight and true into the heart-pine wood. He was, after that, always there when we needed him. Sometimes another job would engross him. Sometimes illness overtook him. But he never told us he couldn't come. He always said, "I'll be there atter while."

The thing that made him especially dear to me as a handyman was that he never belittled or ridiculed my most impractical ideas. Tearing down and moving and reassembling Mr. Henry Troutman's old corncrib did not strike him as a highly impractical task. He was, as he said from the first, willing. And nobody who has moved into a falling-down log cabin will ever underestimate the value of a workman who is willing. When we got another cabin and stuck it onto the first one, he was there on the job, moving with a sort of timeless, tireless deliberation.

When I walk over the yard everything reminds me of my late neighbor. The zigzag rail fence is there because he went over to Mr. Troutman's place off Upper Hembree road and tore down his fence and brought it to my yard and reassembled it.

The round seat around the apple tree is

there because one day on a whim I mentioned that I'd like one. He liked it too. As he finished it, he wiped his brow with his blue bandana and took his seat on it.

"Much time as I've spent here holping you," he remarked, using the Elizabethan pronunciation of *help*, "this is the first time I've had a place to set down."

We needed him and we depended on him. But more than that, we admired him. He was a man with an enormous patience with the human race. I never heard him say an unkind word about anybody. He'd had hard times and trouble, as much as any man, but he was never bitter or blue or critical. He knew how to rest himself and to find escape when he needed it. He took his fishing pole and headed for the creek bank.

Like many a mountain-bred man, he like a frolic, and I remember watching in amazement at one of our community gatherings when he took to the floor and danced to fiddle and guitar music with astonishing lightness and grace. He liked a good story and he could tell one, laughing as hard as anybody if it happened to be on himself.

Sometimes you hear people bemoan the passage of greatness and maybe we don't have all the heroes that we need. But I think there's more danger in overlooking greatness when it is close at hand. Quinton Johnson had a measure which those of us who were his neighbors will long miss.

Windowsills

A young couple is building a new house in our area and one of the things they are proudest of is that it doesn't have a windowsill to its name.

"Not even in the kitchen?" I asked, unbelieving.

"Especially not in the kitchen," the young wife told me proudly. "Everything flush. No place for clutter, you see."

She is a crisp and efficient young woman and I can't believe that she would tolerate untidiness in any form. But not have a kitchen windowsill? What will she do for a laboratory, an art gallery, a nursing home for ailing plants? Where will she put the rocks she picks up on walks? The arrowheads? The bits of fern and moss, the sea shells and cattails, the jug of glycerine she is going to preserve beech leaves in, the snippets of paper which contain addresses, recipies, jokes? She most certainly isn't a messy and avaricious collector of bottles — I'm not either — but when you find a faded, watery-blue jug around an old house site and want to see how it looks with a pink rose in it, where do you put it if you don't have a windowsill?

Until I got my plastic greenhouse I had absolutely no place but the kitchen windowsill to start seedlings. As with country people from time immemorial, the windowsill was the heart of my gardening operation. Here the stuff we determined to hold over from summer to summer maintained a frail, pale green hold on life, getting a little stalky and anemic looking as the winter wore on. Here we kept ferns and geraniums and the hanging baskets with their winter-brown lining of moss and trailing ribbons of wandering Jew. The little ferns from the creek bank of course rejected the whole idea and shriveled up. The coleus, a gaudy, showy medley of color in the summertime, might look a little embarrassed as one who has lingered too long at a party, and tried to make up for it by fading into a self-effacing, muted green.

The begonia, which bloomed tirelessly all the months it hung under the well house, came to the windowsill and quit. The pot of birdsfoot ivy, which I considered indestructible, came down with some mysterious malady which caused it to languish and go limp around the edges.

There were times when the whole idea of saving anything seemed a futile waste of time. But then February comes and the white hyacinths you planted in pebbles and water, kept in the closet under the stairs for weeks, and then moved to the windowsill suddenly begin to bloom. And it all seems worthwhile.

I know why poets carry on about hyacinths. I know the reason for the oft-quoted line about sacrificing a loaf of bread to buy a hyacinth to feed the soul. Mrs. Herb Hawkins up at the seed store is the one who assured me I couldn't fail with hyacinths and, although I figured she didn't know my capacity for failure, I was persuaded. And now I wish I had bought three hundred bulbs and staggered the planting time all through the winter so I'd never be without a couple of white hyacinths in bloom.

They are waxy perfection, pure white clusters of bloom emerging from the satiny fold of green, and their fragrance is heavenly. I move them from windowsill to windowsill to get the maximum pleasure out of the drama of their unfolding.

Hyacinths make you believe in spring. Even as you hover over the hot-air register and look at the ice on the birdbath and the white frost riming the feeder, you see evidence of spring.

If you have room for it you can lean your arms on the windowsill while you wait for coffee in the morning and see the wild plum's fat white buds along every branch, the forsythia by the terrace, and the flowering quinces coming into bloom.

The windowsill is the vantage point from which to find daffodils in sheltered places, a vinca blossom or two, house leeks sending up diminutive rosettes of green, like plump little cabbages.

And one fine day when spring has truly come you can sweep the windowsills clear of everything but the wan and discouraged looking pot plants. No longer will you feel like a proprietor of a rest home for puny plants, the operator of a horticultural hospital. Instead, if they have held out that long, you will have had your own Operation Headstart.

I can't imagine a house without a windowsill.

Kindred Spirits

Sometimes I marvel at the things which constitute a bond between two human beings. Mutual interest, sure, a love of the same things, of course. But occasionally I wonder if mutual prejudice and mutual weakness aren't as strong.

One of my best friends was a woman I merely admired from a distance until I discovered that we had a mutual weakness. She was a doctor's wife and a mover and shaker in the field of education — so intelligent and so capable she intimidated me somewhat, although she was warm and outgoing and clearly wanted to be my friend.

The day I really began to feel close to her was the day she told me over the telephone that she hadn't sent her son to school.

"We are sanding the floors," she said, "and I couldn't find his shoes."

From that moment on, Margaret Bridges and I became best friends. I always admired her for her strengths but I guess I loved her for her weaknesses. She did many things to get our school system to recognize and pay attention to gifted children, and I faithfully went to her meetings and took on whatever assignments she gave me. But the bit of her wisdom that I cherish and remember best was a warning to me not to "go against your nature."

A couple of her children were in college and were coming home for the holidays one year when Margaret, not at all a domestic type, decided to personally take all the old wax off the floors of her house and put down new. She labored on her hands and knees for days and thought she was doing pretty well until she noticed the living-room floor had turned white. She looked at the bottle from which she was getting what she thought was floor wax and it was window cleaner.

"I should have known better," she said bitterly. "It's not my nature to clean house — and I went against it."

To bolster that argument she had the case of the car keys.

It was her "nature" Margaret said, to drop her car keys wherever she happened to be — on the sofa, back of the coffeepot, on the toilet tank in the bathroom, between the pages of whatever book she was reading. The family had one of those key boards in its back hall, but nobody ever used it. One weekend, however, when Margaret was going down to Augusta to see her mother, Dr. Bridges was going to put his car in the shop and she planned to leave her car for him to use in her absence. She put the keys on the board in the back hall.

Poor Glenn," Margaret remarked later. "He looked for the keys all weekend — under sofa cushions and in books and in the bathroom. He finally had to take a taxi."

It did not, of course, occur to him that the keys would be on the key rack in the back hall.

"Proof," Margaret reiterated darkly, "proof that you shouldn't go against your nature."

There's a woman I used to see at the state capitol and admire for her chic appearance and the skill and intelligence with which she lobbied for things ecological. We smiled at one another when we met and spoke cordially when we had a few minutes together outside a committee room or while waiting for an elevator. But our friendship didn't get under way until she brought sandwiches and urged me to share them with her in the sunshine on the capitol lawn one day.

"You know I discovered that we are kindred spirits," she told me. "I saw you drop your pocketbook on the bus the other day, spilling everything in it up and down the aisle. Such a mess . . . and your face was so red! I knew then that we are the same kind of people."

It's an odd bond but a valid one as it turned out. As people who have been in adversity together know, it's easy to draw near one another in hospital waiting rooms, if the building where you have lived or worked together has burned down, and, of course, during wartime shortages and threats and times of grief and mourning.

Even bad weather creates a kind of fellowship which I enjoy. Those who wait out a thundershower in a doorway or under an awning may have met and passed on the street for years without even looking at one another, much less speaking. But trap them together in a downpour and they will smile and talk and eventually share an umbrella or divide a section of damp newspaper so that it will protect two heads instead of one.

Sometimes, however, an unexpected moment of good fortune unites strangers briefly.

One day some time ago I was driving along brooding on something our staff expert on disaster and devastation had written. The living creature, he observed, with the best natural equipment for surviving atomic fallout is the chicken. I was not taking that well because, although I like chicken to eat all right, I consider them messy, self-centered, clattery creatures who normally run the gamut from flustered to panicked. I felt that it was grossly unfair that nature should gear a fool chicken for staying alive in a world which it has never really appreciated.

In such a mood I stopped by my favorite nursery, run by the family of our neighbor Donald Hastings. It wasn't that I needed anything particularly but that I wanted to mooch around seed racks and slat houses for a few minutes, breathing in the fragrance of freshly watered shrubs and little pots of herbs and perhaps talking a bit with garden-minded people with loam on their hands and weather on their minds.

The late Charles Hudson, who for years had written on gardening for our Sunday newspaper and had authored one or two gardening books, passed by and paused to speak. We had just embarked on good talk of seed and rain when a cascade, an avalanche, a crystal tide of birdsong filled the room.

Mr. Hudson turned around to see where it was coming from. All through the store, clerks and customers stopped their transactions and listened.

The notes poured out, filling the big room with melody so clean and joyful it wrenched your heart.

"A mockingbird out there on a rafter at the edge of the roof," a reconnoitering clerk reported.

I tiptoed over to look and there he was — the impeccable mocker, neat, understated, unflamboyant in silver-gray. He had his back to the door where I stood and he sang looking out on a patch of lawn and trees and a street full of heedless motorists beyond.

If he saw me he was unperturbed. He sang on with composure and then he ran an ecstatic arpeggio and was gone. All of us in the store smiled at one another with the tentative warmth of strangers who have been briefly and unexpectedly happy together.

And I felt better about chickens because maybe nature has similarly equipped the mockingbird to survive. Of all God's creatures he would bring the most to a world with its back to the wall.

Bicycles

The person who said Christmas is too good for children wasn't necessarily a cynic. Some things which are normally associated with childhood are better if they come to your later in life. I'm thinking of bicycles.

As a country child living in the piney-woods country of south Alabama, where the roads were deep rutted sand, I never thought to want a bicycle. I'm sure children in the city had them but, as I recall, they were always older boys and I don't remember ever knowing anybody who got one for Chirstmas.

But when my own children came along a bicycle became Santa Claus's number-one priority. My son Jimmy was in the first grade and we were living in a fishing camp out from Orlando when he got his first bicycle. It was a major item for Santa Claus that year and for a time it altered the way of life for all of us. We couldn't do anything else until Jimmy learned to ride, and I spent many an afternoon trotting along beside the new Chrstmas bicycle, holding it steady while its owner pedaled desperately.

The day he sailed off on his own, riding straight and true down the side of the road, I felt like a mother eagle who had just seen her baby eaglet soar from the aerie. I watched the leggy little redhead toil up the slight inclines they have in orange-grove country and zip down them — at first tense and a little fearful and then with increasing confidence and finally no-hands, feet-on-the-handlebars, and I was caught up in the bicycle fever.

Everybody should have one, I knew. But we had many bicycles to go before I ever got my own. Susan turned ten and had to have one for Christmas. For her ninth birthday Mary got a pretty good secondhand one. At twelve Jimmy had a new Schwinn, and when he was fourteen English bicycles with gears were the thing. We awakened one Christmas morning to find both Jimmy and bicycle missing. He had checked out Santa Claus's loot at 4 A.M., found the bicycle, boarded it, and toured the sleeping city in the predawn darkness.

Later he and a friend, who had been similarly endowed by Santa Claus, took off with sandwiches for a day at Stone Mountain, eight miles away. It seemed to me that a bicycle was the most liberating machine I had ever heard of. You needed nothing but it and your own arms and legs to carry you like the wind anywhere you wanted to go. I used to stand on the porch and watch my children and their friends ride up from the park, where they had been to swim, or the library with a basketful of books, and I admired and envied both their skill on their brightly painted steeds and their freedom to move around our town swiftly and at will. My own movements were either by foot — not very fast — or by bus, which placed me at the mercy of transit-company schedules and routes and involved some little money. (Later, when we got a car, it involved more money, of course.)

Looking back it seems that my children had hardly stopped riding their bicycles before they were learning to drive and then owning old cars, then better cars, then getting married and having children who were suddenly ready for bicycles. And we had come full circle, so fast I don't remember when or how the grandchildren learned to ride. It seems to me that they sprang into their bicycle saddles, competent, even showy riders, from the beginning.

At one time my son-in-law Edward managed to outfit four of the children, himself, and his wife, Susan, with bicycles from parts of old ones people gave him or they picked up from trash piles in front of suburban doorways. Their small living room was a mess while Edward was in this bicycle phase with chains and fenders and wheels and a litter of greasy tools spread over everything. But their two little boys, John and Ted, and their cousins Bird and Tib still talk of the summer evenings when the six of them went for long bicycle rides together. They all remember with pride that they had *good* bikes which hardly cost anything besides the paint, which they themselves helped Edward apply.

All this time I was an interested, admiring, and somewhat envious spectator. I knew better than to dream of riding a bicycle because I had already found out to my astonishment that I couldn't water-ski, which I figured would be a snap if I ever got around to it, and I had spent some traumatic hours on icy ski slopes in the north Georgia mountains finding out that I couldn't do that either. (It had looked so easy, too.) I had even been thrown by horses, so I knew better than to think I'd know how to handle a bicycle.

Then one Easter Sunday my friend Jack showed up with a brand-new five-speed bicycle for me.

"You're always talking about how much fun a bicycle tour of England would be," he said. "I got you this on sale so you can learn to ride."

It was the prettiest thing I had ever seen

in a lifetime of looking at other people's bicycles. I walked around it and stroked it and propped it against the stone coping of the well and sat on its neat little saddle, but I didn't have any more idea than a goose how to ride it.

Jack had worked that out. There was the perfect slope at the edge of the yard, he said, fast at the top but tapering off to a long flat, grassy plain. All I had to do was to mount my glittering contraption and hang fast to the handlebars while somebody steadied me and gave me a slight shove over the bank. Moving, the bicycle would stay upright and so, perforce, would I. At the bottom of the bank it wobbled and fell and so did I. But it was a slow, cushioned fall and did me no harm.

My grandchildren delightedly got into the act, holding me up and launching me and shouting words of encouragement as I sailed with increasing steadiness down the bank, slowing to a stop and even braking at the bottom. But I had not tried pedaling and the day I was to check into the hospital for a minor throat operation

Bird and Tib came to the country to "wish me off," as they put it, with a lesson in pedaling down a level stretch of road.

We took off down the firm dirt and gravel road with one on either side of me, holding the bicycle up, pushing to give it momentum and yelling, "Pedal, 'Tine, pedal!" I pedaled wildly, my bike broke from their grasp and was off down the road under its and my power alone! I felt absolutely airborne — just for a second before I realized that I was in truth balancing and pedaling and riding my bicycle by myself. Then I fell.

With a mighty wham bike and I went down in an ignominious heap on the dirt road. Later, in the hospital when they prepared me for my throat operation, the nurses were to wonder at the vast areas of purple and black epidermis covering me.

But I was hooked on bike-riding and I still am. It seems to me to be the most sensible mode of transportation in this mechanized age — quiet and inexpensive and as fast as it need be. Most of the year I get in several bike rides a week, daily if possible. When I am in my mother's little town I try to take my bicycle along for the convenience of quick trips to post office and store and for the pleasure of late-afternoon junkets down a long smooth dirt road which crosses the creek and winds through a forest of magnolia, bay, swamp myrtle, and live oak trees to the lake. There's a small waterfall where I get off and sit a moment, enjoying the sound of the water and the scents of fern and sweet bay.

At home my son and I have pedaled to the little community of Mountain Park three miles away and rested on the dock at the edge of the lake, enjoying the sunset and a beer before pedaling home again. We have a plastic carrying case, which fits exactly in the basket my Long Island friend Mary Hedges gave me for my handlebars and is just right for a couple of cold drinks and sandwiches. There's an old cemetery a few miles in another direction which we love to visit and my grandchildren's favorite place of all — a rock on a bluff overlooking the river. The road is rough and uphill much of the way, so I spend a lot of time pushing my bike, but somehow that makes the time of easy sailing all the more delicious.

Sometimes I really believe my skill as a bicyclist is increasing — nowhere near a match for my children's or grandchildren's, of course. And in any case I don't brag because I nearly always have at least one wrenched or scabby knee, one blue-black elbow, to prove pride doth indeed go before a fall.

I am also well aware that my muscles and my wind have probably not kept pace with even the little skill I have acquired. So I no longer dream of a bike trip through the Cotswolds.

But when I come home from work in the city, shuck my office clothes and shoes, and put on sneakers and an easy old skirt and trundle my bicycle out of the shed, I am filled with a sense of well-being. To be out and moving easily and rapidly under the sky is exhilarating. To shift a gear going downhill and feel the pedals catch and then move smoothly and responsively under my feet fills me with a sense of competence. With the wind in my hair and the sun on my back, I am caught up in self-amazement like the old woman in the fable, crying, "La, me, can this be I?" I cannot ski, I cannot sing. My driving and my dancing are kamikaze feats. But, by gosh, I can ride a bicycle and isn't it fun?

Books

The dream of all reading children, I suppose, is to live in a house with a million books. After you learn to read, your greatest fear is that you will run out of printed words and be left with nothing within miles except the labels on tomato cans and aspirin bottles. I shared this dream and this fear as a child.

To my surprise I learned to be glad that the house where I grew up was not a treasure trove of the world's greatest literature because, like hunger before a bountiful meal, my appetite for books was sharpened and accentuated by the scarcity and uncertainty of the supply.

A smart and funny friend taught me that. The youngest of a college professor's big, bright, and boisterous family, she despised books because she was surrounded by them. She used to yearn, she said, for something to *do* and her impatient father would roar, *"Do? Read!"* and he would wave his hand at the shelves of gloomy-looking books. "There's the Harvard Classics. *Read!"*

She looked at the dark and unpromising covers and opted for a life of illiteracy. The miracle to me was that she got through college and even went back and took her master's degree, avoiding books like the plague every step of the way. She tried a book once, she said, and that was enough. When I heard the title I wasn't surprised that she had renounced books forever. It was Lloyd C. Douglas's *White Banners*.

If I had been in her family I would have read the Harvard Classics because they were there. I would have read *anything*. As an only child, living in the country, I early found that a book could supply me with playmates, take me on trips, open doors to castles, caves or Indian council chambers, let me be in imagination anything I wanted to be. A book gave me what I hungered for most — company.

The trouble lay in getting books. The library at the two-room grammar school was a four-foot shelf of castoffs from a bigger school which had burned. I went through those pretty fast. When you have to walk three miles to school you soon learn to read as you walk. (This is one of my better skills even today. I can traverse a crowded city street without taking my eyes off the printed page and without colliding with more than one person every three blocks.) I remember the Deerslayer as being so real I expected him to pop out of the bushes as I crossed the creek. When I hit Robert Louis Stevenson's *Kidnapped* I was certain ruffians would shanghai me at the next bend in the road.

There was a lot of junk in that collection at school, old and tedious novels like *The Mill on the Floss,* but I plowed doggedly through them, beginning at the top shelf and working down, and occasionally I struck it rich as on the day I reached *Little Women*. That lovely book and all the Alcott books, which I eventually found, became friends for life.

But even if I hadn't gone through it, the school library was not available in the summertime for those endless drowsy hot afternoons for which books were made. I could borrow books — one at a time — from my father's uncle's shelves, if I was careful to approach them with clean hands and a pure heart. Looking back, I wonder why I bothered. He had a great murky unabridged early edition of *Uncle Tom's Cabin* with ugly steel engravings and impossible dialect, and I read and wept and sneezed over the dusty pages of that old book for a solid month. When I took it back and was free to make another selection I looked for something with a bright jacket and bigger print. (Pictures were out of the question. Uncle Lyles' books were pictureless.) I lucked into a goodie expounding Darwin's theory of evolution, which my father made me return. If we were descended from apes, he thought I was too young to know it. I swapped that one for a doctor book, which did have a few pretty graphic line drawings, and my mother made me take that back. I eventually settled on a shelf of old novels and spent a full summer brooding over love among the British upper classes and trying to construct for myself in the chinaberry tree a castle with a tower from which to greet my lover if he came riding.

The public library in Mobile was a far better source but eighteen miles away over roads that got pretty bad in the rainy seasons. In fact we took it for granted that there would be certain stretches of mud through which we would have to be towed by a mule team. So we didn't lightly and whimsically run to town for a book. We planned. We made lists and when we had sufficient errands piled up to justify the expenditure of a dollar for gas, we went. This was usually a Saturday trip and the dime stores and the movies took a portion of the day.

My father was friends with the owners of most of the theaters in Mobile, so we had passes and I seldom missed an installment of the Saturday cowboy serials. While I sat on the front row frozen with suspense over whether Ruth Roland would escape from a blazing railroad car, my mother and a friend would go off to the Bijou to look at what I scorned as "an old love picture," usually starring John Gilbert or Norma Talmadge. But before we went home we went by the library and exchanged last week's five books for five new ones.

This was glorious bounty — for a little while. But when you start reading before you get out of the library door and read all the way home you are well into your supply the first day and you have to ration yourself the rest of the week. My mother took care of that. She didn't exactly consider reading in the morning immoral but she acted as if she did. If you picked up a book before noon you might not pick up the house, much less an iron or a broom or a skillet.

So she decreed that we work in the morning and read only after the midday dinner dishes were done. And what wonderful, faithful friends I made on those summer afternoons — Anne of

Green Gables and the Little Colonel, Pollyanna and Rebecca of Sunnybrook Farm, Page Allison and the Tucker twins, Mrs. Wiggs, the Little Peppers, all the fairy stories and that great gilded company of Roman and Greek gods and goddesses. (Sometimes I wince at the ludicrous sight I must have presented when I made the beds in the morning, wrapping myself in a sheet and parading around as Athena, the goddess of wisdom. It was hard on the sheets but it sure enlivened bed-making.)

They say a mother who makes illness pleasant for a child is fostering hypochondria and I'm afraid my mother risked that without having ever heard the word. When I had a cold or malaria's chills and fevers, which everybody in south Alabama expected to have in those days, the rule against reading in the morning was lifted. I could read all day long if I felt up to it, and if I was weak or too tired to read to myself my mother would sometimes pull up a rocker and read to me. I remember the particularly happy convalescence from pleurisy when I was bundled up in a quilt before the fire and my mother read long narrative poems to me all afternoon. The wind blew, the rain sluiced down the windowpanes, and we were off in the forest primeaval with Longfellow's Evangeline or shipwrecked with Tennyson's Enoch Arden. There was one moving poem about the misspent life of a Lady Hildegard, which I loved and lost and have never been able to find since. But it was so powerful that when we had worn it out with reading we assembled my dolls, made them clothes like the English gentry, and played out the poem.

Because poor health has so many other things against it I think I avoided hypochondria all right, but when illness does come I know how to make the most of it — read. I would rather leave my nightgown and toothbrush at home when I check into a hospital than to leave behind my basket of books. I don't remember the pain of childbirth — who does? — but I do associate the birth of my daughter Mary with *The Robe.* I was reading it the night the labor pains began and I could hardly bear to go to the delivery room without it.

As soon as she made her appearance and I was conscious again I grabbed the book and finished it. Then I was wild to get a Bible and check out the source of some things that were in the fictionalized account. My husband went out to an open-all-night drug store and brought me a ninety-eight-cent red-letter edition, which engrossed me during the rest of my hospital stay.

Later I happened to be in Hollywood when they were filming *The Robe* and I'll never forget the Jewish press agent who took me to see the sets. We came to the three crosses on the hill and he said, "Here we have Gethsemane."

"Don't you mean Golgotha?" I asked.

He shrugged. "Maybe so," he said. "I didn't read the book."

One of the happiest recoveries from flu I ever had was when I reread *Gone with the Wind*. The first time I read it I didn't live in Atlanta, and it meant a lot, when I read it the second time, to have known the author and to be able to place the roads and streets and the little towns in it.

The nuns at St. Joseph's Infirmary in

Atlanta are friends, and when I have been a patient there they have improved my lot immeasureably with books from their library and personal collections. The tedium of tests and X-rays was eased for me by *Jonathan Livingston Seagull* and a Gladys Tabor book on flower arranging the last time I was in St. Joseph's.

The practical use of books is one I didn't know about until I got old enough to hit the how-to section of the Girl Scout manual, but it is a side on which I have leaned heavily over since. In recent years my collections of cookbooks and gardening manuals have grown faster than my shelves of novels for the reason that a how-to book can be used over and over again and few novels are keepers.

Atlanta's longtime mayor William B. Hartsfield, one of the most progressive, imaginative, and colorful mayors the city ever had, always called himself a graduate of Carnegie Library. He grew up at a time when his family could not spare his help long enough for him to work his way through college. He had not heard the poet Robert Frost's theory that when you learn to read the need of formal education has been met, but he thought reading might help. So he wrote letters to a dozen college presidents throughout the country, asking them for a list of the ten books they regarded as most valuable. Then he began to read. He read every book on every list — and if a book showed up twice in the list, he read it twice.

Mr. Hartsfield was a richly educated man and a wit besides. I happened to be in his office one day when a movie press agent arrived unexpectedly with a talking horse who was on a personal appearance tour. Would he welcome the horse to the city?

"Gladly," said Mr. Hartsfield, walking toward microphones and cameras.

"This is the first time," he said warmly, "that I have had the pleasure of welcoming a *whole* horse to my office."

Louis L'Amour, the best-selling author, is another man who lacked formal education but read himself into a prodigious knowledge of world history and literature. He once told me that you cannot begin reading early enough. The day his children were brought home from the hospital, newborn infants, he began the daily ritual of reading to them, a practice he has pursued since. When they were babies he read poetry to them, believing that they caught the rhythm of the lines and the music of the words. Now that they are teen-agers he meets them at the breakfast table with whatever interests him at the moment — a bit of research, something he is writing, a novel, a history, outdoor lore. As a result his children are omnivorous readers themselves.

When I hear of organized, purposeful readers I regret my own haphazard reading. There's so much I haven't read, so much I don't even know about. But then I think of the good books I have lucked into, the books which have faithfully stood by me when I needed to know how to do something or the wonderful, life-expanding books I have stumbled onto, when I most needed them, and I am overwhelmed with gratitude to them and their authors.

Riding to Work

Friends who live in the city sometimes deplore the fact that I have moved thirty miles out in the country and am prone to go home at night instead of to some of the more stimulating parties, lectures, and concerts. One friend, who dwells in a high-rise apartment practically downtown, thinks I waste a lot of time commuting.

"There's only so much you can do with one life," she points out. "Why waste two hours a day on a highway?"

The scarcity of time is a plague to everybody, of course, and when I look around at the piled-up, neglected, started-and-unfinished, and just-dreamed-of-doing things, I am likely to wonder if my life style doesn't need new management.

In a push toward putting some order in my life, toward saving money and time, I have taken to parking my car in the little town of Roswell, six miles away from my house, and catching the bus to town. And although it might not accomplish all the things I have set for it, this bus riding is lovely.

What I had not realized was how companionable it is, compared to driving alone in your car. Driving a car on the freeway, you develop a sort of instinctive hostility toward the human race, I suppose. People in the other cars are dehumanized. On a bus the other passengers are seen close up and your sense of kinship is re-established.

The bus driver on our run was a local boy, reared on a farm up the road near Alpharetta, and he knows many of the passengers by their names. He is careful with the parade of oldsters going into town to the hospital or the doctor, and I have seen him pull up his bus and park and get out and take a blind woman across the street to a stop where she will catch a transfer bus to her Golden

Age handcraft class.

You find yourself wondering about the other passengers. The waitress in her crisp uniform and big rubber-soled shoes is clean and fresh in the morning but, as she cheerfully tells us all, it won't be long till she has gravy stains on her apron and her feet are hurting.

There's a man in work clothes reading the Help Wanted ads in the paper, and when he gets off downtown you watch him go, wondering how they're doing at his house and hoping he finds something today.

A long-haired kid gets on looking sleepy and by some remarkable alchemy keeps his eyes closed until a cute little girl with a ruffle over her bottom instead of a skirt gets on the bus. Suddenly he is wide awake and smiling, and within two blocks he had moved up to the seat behind her and is leaning forward to begin a conversation.

Like many people, I think I am going to be wary of striking up conversations on the bus. We all have a built-in device to protect us from boredom, I suppose, and we exhibit it by burrowing deeper into our book or newspaper when a talker sits beside us. The sad thing is we'll never know how much *good* talk we miss that way.

If Mrs. Bailey hadn't have been a neighbor I wouldn't have shared her seat one morning and I would have missed a glimpse of life in our settlement as it was forty-five years ago.

At seventy-odd, Mrs. Bailey is rosy and pretty and strong enough to keep her house, cook company meals, work in her yard, and drive her car everywhere she wants to go. She happened to be riding the bus that day because her feet have been hurting a lot lately, she was on her way to the doctor, and she wanted to avoid having to cope personally with the traffic and worry about parking.

What was her trouble with her feet, I asked.

"Hard work, lots of hard work," she said cheerfully. And then she told me.

For thirty or forty years she worked in the local pants factory and then went home at night and worked in the fields until it was too dark to see. After that she stayed up preparing and canning vegetables — "until the house was so hot we couldn't sleep when we did get to bed."

When she and her husband moved from Atlanta to the old house on the hill down the road from me in 1931, they had almost nothing in common with the young couples who have bought up developer-built ranch houses and pseudo-southern colonial mansions in the subdivision bordering on their old cotton field now.

"We were broke, flat broke," she said. "Harry hated the idea of living in a rented place though, and with both of us working after we were married we bought us a little house near Lakewood in Atlanta. It was cheap and a city house and Harry was raised on a farm and he wanted to go back to it. So we sold the little house and bought land up here."

She smiled at me. "We come with nothing."

An Atlanta doctor lent them $325 for a start, an evidence of faith which still causes her to go misty-eyed when she thinks of it.

"We went down on Decatur Street to a wholesale grocer and bought a can of lard and a barrel of flour to see us through the first year," she remembered, "and we put them in that little back room and nailed the window shut. I was so afraid something would happen to them."

Harry caught a ride to Atlanta, no casual, easy trip in those days of slippery clay roads, and bought a horse, which he rode home, getting in dusty and tired late at night.

The first year's vegetables were a richness and a glory to them, and the corn and cotton crop so good they were able to start repaying the $325 stake. But hard labor never ceased for either of them. They toiled to eat and toiled to stay warm and toiled to pay the doctor bills and buy the medicine for six older members of their family who came at various times to make their home with them. One relative, a widow, arrived to spend a few days while she looked for a place to live, and she stayed for fourteen years.

"We loved every one of them, and help — oh, they were lots of help! Cooked and worked in the fields when they were able and helped me with the canning and washing and ironing. They could fire up that old three-legged black iron pot and boil the clothes as white as you ever saw. Never a lonesome minute when they was about."

The Baileys have outlived the old folks in their family and sometimes their old house on the hill seems big for them. But they like their young neighbors with their subdivision houses and carports full of power mowers and station wagons and boats and boat trailers. They are comfortable themselves. The weather-darkened old house has been covered with aluminum siding painted a cheerful green and cream and equipped with electricity and plumbing.

Mrs. Bailey assembled her bag and umbrella for getting off at the Doctors' Building and smiled at me.

"It's been a long time," she said, "since I sat in front of the fireplace and watched the cold wind come up through the cracks in the floor and make the hearth rug rise up and float.''

The time I save on the bus has not been put to any spectacular use yet but I enjoy it, ah, how I enjoy it.

Even if I take the car I am not sure the time spent driving to and from the office is the barren waste my friends believe. Sometimes it seems to me it's the best part of the day.

There are all kinds of sights on the road — country ones like the bare tree I saw one day by the site where a barn burned down a couple of years ago. The tree was a casualty of the fire, too, life gone, only its scorched black skeleton left. But one morning I passed it and saw that its stark ebony branches were garlanded and festooned with green leaves and a startling snow-white wreath of morning-glory blossoms.

Now if I lived in a high-rise apartment would I have seen that?

Neither would I have been caught in traffic backed up on a ramp leading off the expressway when another woman driver, at the head of the procession, couldn't get up the courage to move out into the intersection. A man in a car behind her and ahead of me put all his weight on his horn, not once but repeatedly. The woman's car stayed put and I could see why. There was a rushing tide of cars in front of her and it looked scary, venturing out there. The man blew his horn once too often.

Suddenly the door of the lead car popped open and the woman got out and stalked back even with her tormentor and sat down on the grassy shoulder of the road.

"If you want it moved, move it yourself!" she cried in a ringing voice. "I've had it."

And she promptly burst into tears.

The impatient man had to get out of his car and move hers across the street to a filling station and come back and get his car. It delighted me that a cacophony of horn-blowing from all the cars backed up behind him greeted him. I consider that one sight memorable.

As for missing all the excitement in the city at night, sometimes I regret it. I'm apologetic to my friends. But it's really awfully nice to go to the woods at the end of a day, especially in the spring.

Sometimes there's still enough light in the sky to see, and I never weary of looking at the greening pastures, particularly when they are adorned with wobbly-legged baby calves. I like to inspect the dooryards where something new is likely to pop into bloom almost every day in April.

When the wild azalea blooms in our woods you can count on a marvelous range of color from airy white to rose to brilliant burnt orange. Roadside banks then are blue with iris and the loveliest violets — the great big ones with lacy leaves and golden hearts which we call birdfoot violets and the botanists call pansy violets. Wild cherry trees will be white with bloom, the pines dusted with gold, and the oaks unfolding tiny rosy leaves that are the velvety texture of a baby's hand.

Even if the light is gone when we turn

off the paved road onto the dirt road leading to Sweet Apple, I can smell the sweet shrub and some delicate indefinable fragrance from the hollow where the muscadines grow.

If it's early enough we have our own little drama to see in the backyard — how it is with the tomatoes, the parsley, and the sage, and whether the new geraniums in the window box are flourishing and the lilies of the valley are blooming.

Even if it is getting dark, it's not bad to stand on the back steps and look at the stars and listen to the whippoorwills. I loved the young one whose voice seemed to be changing because now and then there'd be a break in his call and when he resumed it seemed to me it was in a chastened tone, as with a teen-age boy who has just suffered the humiliation of hearing his new baritone voice go soprano.

It isn't Bernstein or Entremont but I like the murmuring of small birds settling down in the persimmon tree and the stirring of the wind in the pines. Crickets come to life in the weeds out by the road, the little spotted hoptoads venture out from the woodpile for a stroll in the evening dew, and if I'm very quiet I might hear a family of young foxes barking down in the sawdust pile.

Hand-Me-Downs

My eldest granddaughter, Tib, now twelve, really rocked the family recently. All out of a clear sky she said this incredible thing.

"Someday," she told us with a sort of believe-it-or-not air, "I'm going to have some *new* clothes."

"What do you need, honey?" I asked her, concerned.

"It's not that I *need* anything," she said. "I've got a lot of hand-me-downs. I'm talking about going into a store and buying *new* clothes!"

We all looked at her in blank surprise for a minute and then glanced at one another uneasily, seeking reassurance. This wasn't going to be an oddball, a wild and foolish dreamer, was it? Imagine *wanting* new clothes.

There are times, we admit, when it is necessary to go into a store and buy something absolutely unused, unseasoned, even unmarked down. But they are unusual times, compounded of crises and desperation. Would she choose to do it? What could be wrong with this maverick child of ours?

"Talk to her, Mother," my daughter whispered to me. "Tell her about Thoreau and Carlyle and the women of Boston."

So I tried. I merrily recounted the Cleveland Amory tale of the rich and plain women of Boston, who considered it tacky to go around rigged out in the latest fashion. It bespeaks a flighty, unstable character and, even worse, new money. The good line is, of course, that one about hats.

Somebody, according to Mr. Amory, looked at the battered headgear these ladies wore (they probably don't today) and asked where they got their hats.

"Where do we get our hats?" repeated a grande dame in surprise. "Why, we *have* our hats!"

Our little girl laughed but she wasn't converted, I could tell. Neither was she impressed by Thoreau's "Beware of enterprises requiring new clothes." I had to look up Carlyle to get his line straight. "Trust not the heart of that man for whom old clothes are not venerable."

Tib was not sure what venerable was, and when I explained she wasn't really turned on by it. But I was and I set to thinking all over again about all the joys of hand-me-downs. As a Depression-era child, I grew up in many a made-over from friends and relatives. When we look at snapshots in old albums my mother and I frequently admire the clothes.

"That's a cute dress you're wearing," she will say about a plaid wool of my tenth year. "I made it from a skirt Aunt Ida gave me."

Or, "Didn't that blouse turn out well? The goods came from a dress Miss Perkins backed up to the fire and scorched behind. I ripped it apart and made it over."

One of the memorable windfalls of my childhood was what we referred to as "Aunt Talley's Box." Aunt Talley was my father's oldest aunt and she had made family history in her youth by marrying a Yankee and going Up North to live. The Yankee husband died, and Aunt Talley got a job of some kind and the family heard very little from her until the days of the Depression, when she cleaned out her attic and sent us The Box.

Such loot, such gorgeous loot!

Everything in the box was a costume of the 1880s or '90s, apparently of the time when Aunt Telley was newly married and well off. There were dresses with sweeping skirts and leg-o'-mutton sleeves and hundreds of tiny covered buttons down the front. There were lace collars and jabots and taffeta petticoats. All of them bore the label of what we conceived to be a stylish Chicago ladies' tailor.

My mother had a marvelous time ripping seams and steaming and pressing and making suits and skirts and jumpers by 1930s patterns out of the old and elegant fabrics. But there was one garment she couldn't manage to make over — a long black coat of the kind people in stories called "great" coats. It, too, had leg-o'-mutton sleeves and the wool, designed for Chicago weather, seemed richer and finer than any we had seen in south Alabama. It was lined in pearly white satin and ornamented with opulent black braid. It was a shame to cut it up, Muv said, and she really couldn't fit any of her patterns to its adroitly curved seams if she had wanted to. We had a vague idea that it should be preserved, but in those days there was no vogue for the quaint and old-fashioned. So we ended up hanging the coat by the back door for use by anybody going out in the weather. It became known by the name of its donor, Aunt Talley, and to this day I can hear my mother say, "Take Aunt Talley and run down to the commissary for me," or "Put on Aunt Talley and bring in a basket of rosin chips for the fire." Even my father would sling Aunt Talley over his shoulders if he had to go out in the yard in the rain or cold at night.

Aunt Talley was warm, nearly waterproof, and she had personality. Which is, I have found, true of many clothes which have come to us the hand-me-down route. I raised my children in the clothes of Harold Martin's children, and although many years have elapsed since she she received it, my mother still cherishes and saves for the hospital a particularly handsome bed jacket which belonged to Boyce Martin's late mother.

"If I should need it," she said during a recent hospital stay, "I've still got my good Martin wrapped in tissue paper in that top drawer."

My favorite housecoat, a soft and worn old blue number now of a venerable age, is called Julia — for the friend who gave it to me. Two striped jerseys out of L. L. Bean by way of our friend Larry are worn by any member of the family who happens to be chilly and in need of something light and warm to slip on. They are called, of course, Larrys. The most spectacularly successful dress my daughter Susan had as a child was blue gingham ruffled from waist to hem and selling in our smartest junior shop at a fantastic twenty-five dollars. Even now, when the simplest dress for her baby can cost twice that, Susan speaks dreamily of the blue ruffled gingham as "my Lucy Bridges," given to her by the friend of that name.

There is a difference, I like to think, between hand-me-downs and castoffs. A garment from a friend is likely to have already had a season or two of being well-loved and enjoyed and is passed on to you because you are the kindred spirit who will love and enjoy it too. The bestowal of hand-me-downs from the Martins used to be one of our favorite spring and fall rites. They didn't drop off a box of worn and stained old discards. Instead, Mrs. Martin, called Pokey by her friends, would call up and invite us to "come by and try on."

There before the commodious closet in their back bedroom we would inspect, admire, and choose. Everything Mrs. Martin gave us was of recent vintage — one or two years old at most — and newly dry-cleaned, waiting for us in rustling grandeur in plastic bags. Far from feeling underprivileged, my children rejoiced in the windfalls, preening and parading and telling everybody about their good fortune.

That is not the case with people who have to take unwanted discards, I know. Once I wrote a column about my family's pleasure in hand-me-downs and was astonished at some of the bitter and unhappy experiences people related. One woman, a minister's daughter, felt shamed at having to wear the clothes of the daughter of her father's richest parishioner.

"Everything she had was purple," the woman wrote, "and me with pink hair. I looked like a bad case of impetigo."

To her the clothes had malevolent personalities, if any. To us they bear the names and a certain likeness to friends. New clothes are all right. You get them when you have to. But they are not very interesting. There's nothing to say about them. No story to tell. They are hybrids of unknown lineage. Not until they take on the patina of age and become trusted and comfortable old friends can they really hold their own with the standbys of the family.

I'm not really worried about my granddaughter Tib. She's a good, biddable child. I'm sure we can teach her.

Reminders

Reminders are great things, particularly for those of us with capricious, self-serving memories. I'm not talking about calendars and memo pads, which remind you of appointments and tasks, although they are certainly useful to me — if I can remember to write things down ahead.

I am not even talking about those little daily readings which I like very much and in which I often find what the Sunday-school books used to call "Our Lesson for Today."

The reminders which are the true blessings lift your spirits when you are low, ease your ego when it has had a walloping blow, return you to the company of real people when you feel guilty and unworthy, jack you up and restore you to sanity when you are evil-tempered, self-pitying, or self-righteous.

Just as a seed catalogue is a reminder of spring in the dead of winter, a note or a phone call is a reminder that you have friends and are loved when you are low. And the minute you feel superior to somebody else you are lucky if some reminder of their strength and your own weakness hits you.

You would think if there is anybody you might feel superior to it's a man under life sentence for murder, and I suppose I wore my personal rectitude like a mantle when I went to interview one in the local jail many years ago.

He was a man who had been wanted in Atlanta for murder for twenty years before some vacationing officers saw and recognized him on a golf course in California in the 1940s. He had been brought back, tried, and convicted and had served several years of a life sentence when I first heard of him. The city editor told me that a man known as the "Bunco

King" had tried to kill himself. He sent me to Fulton Tower, the then county jail, to talk to him.

I suppose I expected some brute of a man, a gangster type who had gunned down a rival gambling kingpin in a hotel corridor back in the 1920s. The man I met in the prison cell was slender, almost ascetic looking, with a shock of white hair, bright blue eyes, a soft voice, and a diffident, gentle way of speaking. He didn't want any more publicity, but he didn't know how to turn down a young woman who had gone to the trouble to come and see him. Finally, to avoid talking to me, he showed me a letter he had been reading from his wife.

She had heard he was in the hospital (they hadn't told her it was a suicide attempt), and she was sad that she had not been able to move a cot into his room and stay by his side as she always had in the past.

Then she went on with details of life at home — the place they had built together in all the years that he had, without her knowing it, been a fugitive. She and their little girl had just come from choir practice, she wrote, and they had a Brownie meeting the next day. Some workmen had come to give them an estimate on fixing the roof. The roses he planted were prettier than they had ever been before. She loved him and missed him.

The man I had automatically dehumanized in my mind because he was a murderer suddenly appeared to me in a different light. His wife's letter had reminded me that there was something more to him, that he had a wife and a child and a garden and a leaky roof, that he loved to work in the earth and had planted roses. Except for that shooting twenty-odd years before, he was a man like any other man with people who loved him and simple, homely things that had occupied him.

It took a while, several years in fact, but I went back into the history of his case and found that there had been mitigating circumstances. There was evidence that he had shot, as he contended, in self-defense. A coroner's jury had held that originally, but its report had been mysteriously lost. I found some of the old jurors and they signed a petition for a parole. I talked to people in the little California town where he had gone to change his name and make a new life for himself, and found that he was one of the most respected and loved men in town. He had worked hard for civic and charitable causes but was best known for his work with troubled teen-agers. A neighbor told me that his workshop in his backyard was a gathering place for kids and by his interest in them and his encouragement he had kept more than one from getting into trouble.

He had done for himself what the prison system in those days couldn't do much about — completely changed his life.

Eventually he won a hearing before the parole board and he was given his freedom. To avoid alerting other reporters, his lawyer and a friend whisked him out of jail and into a private plane for a trip to Memphis, where he would board an airliner for home. They took me with them and I'll never forget the trip. He called his wife from the airport and came out of the booth with a look of surprise and tender amusement on his face.

"Do women always cry when they're happy?" he asked.

It was raining lightly when he made a dash for his plane, but he smiled as he put up a hand to touch the dampness on his shoulders and his head.

"You forget what rain feels like — in *there,*" he said.

Many times in the intervening years I have felt the rain and have been reminded of him and how fortunate and happy he felt to be out in it that late afternoon.

He is dead now, and I have lost touch with his wife and daughter. But I'll always be glad that I knew him and grateful for the lines in his wife's letter which reminded me that he was not a cliché, a murderer, but a man, a good man.

There are reminders which put you in your place when you start to give yourself airs, of course. Most of us probably find it easy to take on the color of our environment, and when I used to go to Hollywood for our paper I found in myself a surprising bent to "go Hollywood," as the expression was in those days. One memorable afternoon I went to the home of the swimming star Esther Williams for an interview and ended up in her pool, dog-paddling along beside her as she did her celebrated Olympic crawl. I felt so at home I could hardly tell the difference between myself and the movie star until we climbed out of the pool.

"Are you wearing one of Esther's suits?" the press agent who had taken me there asked, looking at the statuesque Miss Williams with her big beautiful body and then looking at me.

"Sure," I said smugly.

"She certainly is," Miss Williams said warmly. "One of my maternity suits."

It was a good reminder and just in time because that night I went to a premiere wearing an evening dress Miss Williams had worn in *The Duchess of Idaho*, and I knew exactly who I was and why I was there. Glamour was no part of it.

Another time in Hollywood I went to be "done" by the celebrated makeup artist Wally Westmore at Paramount Studios. Mr. Westmore blotted out my nose and made me a smaller one, raised my cheekbones and enlarged my eyes, gave me long swooping eyelashes and curly hair, and colored me pretty.

I looked so good I toyed with the idea of applying for a screen test before I left the lot. But then I got back to the hotel and looked in the mirror. There stood an utter stranger — a fixed-up stranger.

A wave of homesickness hit me. I was in an impersonal hotel room three thousand miles from home and I didn't even have my familiar, if plain, old face along. I went in the bathroom and stuck my head under the shower. What emerged was a poor thing but mine own.

Children dependably remind you of promises and plans. "You SAID . . ." will pull you up short every time.

A woman reader once wrote in to

remind me of something I had "said" in print, and it caught me at a time when I was feuding with everybody I cared about and was in a high state of self-pity.

She found "so true," she wrote, my contention that we are with the people we love "at best, such a short time that we should not let petty grievances blight any of the time we have."

Did I ever write such a thing, I wondered. I couldn't remember. In my current mood it sure sounded Pollyannaish of me.

Closer to the truth, I thought wearily, would be the line taken by my grandchild Ted when he was six years old. He had written a six-page book, the title of which was *Hate at All Times*. Hatred, I had been thinking, could be a fine sustaining emotion. (Sometimes I think my mother is kept going by a strong streak of rancor.) And, of course, it can also be pure poison.

As I reflected on the lady's letter, serving up to me my own words, I realized that I really lack whatever strength of character it takes to stay angry or to fight with people I love. I may vent my spleen in petty ways but a good walloping war is beyond me. I'm afraid they'll fight back and if they do they'll tell me some unpleasant truths about myself, which I'll be a long time remembering.

Besides that, I don't like to alienate them for more than ten minutes at a time. If they go away mad I miss them too much. The minute they are out of sight I forget whatever reprehensible quality I've just been decrying and remember all the good things — the humor and the fun and some random moment of generosity and understanding.

Here the reminders, bless 'em, get in their licks. A scrap of music, a funny story, a discarded sneaker on the closet floor, the slant of familiar handwriting on an envelope, a telephone number on the kitchen wall. You see and you remember and you can't think what it was that caused you to risk the loss of a friend or relative so dear.

Superstitions

The woman said she just loved Southerners, they are so cute and backward and superstitious. I had a choice of slapping her sassy face (she was smaller than I am), giving her a piece of my mind, or hearing her out. I decided to see what other significant and penetrating observations she had to make.

"You are *colorful!*" she said triumphantly, as if she had sought a long time for just the right adjective and finally found it. "You are just as colorful as . . . as . . ."

"As Joseph's coat," I finished for her. And then threw in gratuitously, "Cute as a speckled pup, too. And barefooted as a yard dog."

"See!" she said. "I told you. Now what I want you to tell me is some of your superstitions. What do you people believe? What do you fear?"

I choked back an impulse to tell her that, like Marilyn Monroe told Dame Edith Sitwell, we believe everything a little bit. And we probably fear everything some too. But doesn't everybody?

Of course Southerners are no more superstitious than other Americans. We may have some different superstitions from English and African forebearers to put up against those which other Americans inherited from German, Russian, Scandinavian, and Oriental ancestors. But I am perfectly sure that Southerners only believe in such superstitions as are convenient and fun.

I don't put a hat on the bed, it's true, but I don't think I am afraid to. Sure, I've always heard it was bad luck and I need all the luck I can get. The bed just isn't a good place for hats, that's all. I don't like to see an unoccupied rocker rocking either. I always put out a hand and stop it. Same with cradles. But I don't really believe having a wild bird loose in the house means there'll be a death in the family. In the country in a log cabin full of open places we practically always have a wren batting in and out.

Why do we preserve our superstitions? If I thought it was out of fear and ignorance I'd never let one creep into a book on blessings, I promise you. I happen to think old superstitions tell us a lot about our ancestors and are marvelously interesting. Maybe it *is* color they bring to the mundane, although I don't offer the word triumphantly. Maybe they offer a little insight into old-time customs and beliefs.

There are some cheerless ones: Touch a dead man's head and he'll never haunt you. The number of cars in a funeral procession are the number of days before the next funeral. The first person to occupy a new graveyard will never "lie sweet" but will be a restless spirit forevermore. Cows lowing at night foretell a death — and so do whippoorwills calling near the house or three white horses seen at once.

The ones I really like the best involve

plants, especially those used in Christmas decorations. A landscape horticulturist at the University of North Carolina, Henry J. Smith, once shared with me a lovely lot of beliefs he collected about our Yuletide greens.

Ancient Druid priests, for instance, never allowed mistletoe to touch the ground but cut it with a golden sickle and caught it in a white cloth, distributing it to their followers, who believed that it brought happiness, romance, and peace. When it grew in oak trees, which seldom happens with the European variety according to Hank Smith, it was supposed to have healing properties and was called by the early Christians "lignum Sanctae Crucis" or "wood of the Holy Cross."

Because of my Scandinavian ancestors I was delighted to hear that in ancient Scandinavia enemies meeting by chance beneath a tree bearing mistletoe were "obliged to disarm, embrace in friendship, and keep peace together for the rest of the day." Mistletoe grows in the persimmon tree back by my driveway and I have always wanted to bring enemies together there and test that theory.

The Romans, Mr. Smith told me, exchanged green tree branches for good luck on the first day of January. The English carried the custom to Christmas, singing:

"Holly and ivy, box and bay
Put in the church on Christmas Day."

There are all kinds of legends about the holly tree and superstitions too. Mr. Smith didn't repeat the one to the effect that the holly tree was used for the cross and thereafter destined to bear thorns. His version was that the leaves were used as the crown of thorns for Christ and thereby compelled to have red berries to symbolize His drops of blood. I believe in hanging holly over the doors at Christmas time but because it's pretty and not because I believe it will protect the household from witches and thunder and lightning, as the superstition has it.

And if I happen to think of it I put a sprig of holly on the beehives as a way of telling the bees Christ was born because it is a nice custom and not because they are not really well-informed bees.

The pretty legends, I'm afraid, are not the ones the lady wanted from Southerners. I had to tell her I had never tied a nutmeg around a baby's neck to prevent colic in my life and we didn't wear silver coins around our ankles to stave off voodoo. But I did put sourwood branches over my child's bed to prevent bronchitis and after all I had been through I would have put an alligator or a buzzard there if I had heard it was helpful.

Plants will never grow if you thank the person who gave them to you, and stolen plants grow best of all. Howling dogs mean death; you'll get warts if you handle toads; company is coming when roosters crow in the middle of the day; if your shoes come untied your sweetheart is thinking about you; throw a kiss to a redbird and you'll see your sweetheart soon; when the fire on your hearth sings it's going to snow.

Many superstitions are said to have been brought from Africa by Negro slaves. One I heard recently was that trash swept out the door at night would bring about the sale of a slave who did the sweeping. As a child I remember hearing that it was bad luck to sweep the floor after sundown but I took it to mean that you were slovenly and inefficient because you should have done it early in the day. Bringing garden tools like a hoe or an axe into the house is terrible luck. If your nose itches, somebody's coming. If you sneeze on Sunday the devil will get you during the week.

If you step over a child who is lying on the floor you'll halt his growth. If you sit on a trunk some ill fortune will befall you. If you sweep under a single person's feet he'll never get married. When you see a cross-eyed person you must quickly cross your fingers — unobtrusively, if possible.

There are plenty of planting superstitions, many of them old English, I believe, like the one about the fertility of soil and vigor of the crops being assured if the planters, male and female, are naked when they sow the seeds.

So far I haven't seen this one tested, but then I haven't really checked up on my farmer neighbors on the moonlight nights in April and May.

Church

I like church.

Some church doctrine bothers me and the vocabulary of the pious is often distressing. Taking into account her sincere concern, the lady who wrote in, asking if I was "saved in the blood of the Lamb," left me feeling disturbed and embarrassed.

But I like church.

There have been great stretches in my life when I haven't been faithful to church. I have wondered . . . and wandered . . . and stayed away for years at a time.

But I like church.

There is a rightness and an order in being in church on Sunday morning. The discipline of getting up and getting there, of sitting in a straight and uncompromising pew with hair combed and face washed and best dress on may be part of it. For some of us there is a certain comfort and security in discipline.

What is known as the order of worship pleases and reassures me. I like — under cover of the choir's mighty voice — to lift my own quavering and tuneless alto in the Gloria. ("Glory be to the Father and to the Son and to the Holy Ghost . . . As it was in the beginning, is now, and ever shall be, world without end . . . Amen, A-amen.") I like, when the collection is taken up, getting to my feet and swinging out with "Praise God from whom all blessings flow!"

I like church.

I like the old hymns, the bouncy tunes of "Amazing Grace" and "Blest Be the Tie That Binds," the stately words and grand organ sounds of Beethoven's Ninth with words by Dr. Henry van Dyke. ("Joyful, joyful we adore thee, God of glory, Lord of love.") My heart lifts to the simulated trumpet sound which opens

"God of Our Fathers, Whose Almighty Hand." (Sometimes on special occasions they have real trumpets in church for this.)

Hymns were the first poetry for some of us who were country bred. Hymns and the Psalms. And who could ask for anything better than "The heavens declare the glory of God; and the firmament sheweth His handywork"? I remember chanting, "Teach me some me-lodious sonnet, sung by angel tongues above," long before I ever read a real sonnet or knew the meaning of the word "melodious."

"Come Thou Fount of Every Blessing" delights me to this day because after many years of puzzling over it I learned the meaning of the words "Here I raise mine Ebenezer." The dictionary doesn't say, but a scholarly Sunday-school teacher, Dorothy Dickens, who had studied Greek, Latin, Hebrew, and some Aramaic, told me an ebenezer was a sort of house flag, a symbol of at-homeness in a strange land. I have mentally raised ebenezers many times since.

The reading of the scriptures before a

hushed and listening body of people moves me. Sometimes I open a pew Bible and follow along as the minister intones the words that are often fresh and strange, occasionally as familiar and full of imagery as these from Isaiah: "He shall feed his flock like a shepherd: he shall gather the lambs in his arm, and carry them in his bosom. . . ."

To a Protestant the sermon is the important part of the service. Our traditions emphasize the teaching role of the minister, rather than the celebration of the ritual. We depend on his sermon to give us new insights into the business of living. We expect from it direction for the week ahead. Eloquent men with the gift of oratory sometimes lift us to surprising heights of service and sacrifice, but more often the sermon merely makes us resolve to try harder and do better.

I like church.

I like the church holidays — Christmas and Easter and Thanksgiving. During the intervals when I have been away from the church my observance of those lovely days of feast and celebration suffered greatly because in my mind they are essentially religious holidays. We can give gifts and sing carols without going to church at Christmas but it is not the same. It's as if the wise men sent their frankincense and gold and myrrh by United Parcel and did not seek out the Babe in the manger. When my children were small the carol service and meditation on Christmas morning were essential to our observance of the day. They did, in fact, establish its mood, and it seemed to me that the stresses and excitements of the rest of the day somehow eased up and the giving-and-getting commotion slipped into its proper perspective.

This service at North Avenue presbyterian church in Atlanta is so important a part of the church year that members and the longtime minister, Dr. Vernon S. Broyles, Jr., have preserved it in the face of considerable difficulties. During World War II Christmas Day 1942 dawned to find Atlanta encased in ice — the worst ice storm in the city's history.

The streets were slick and hazardous, power lines and some trees were down. Planes, trains, trolleys, and buses were at a standstill. Nothing anywhere moved.

At the old gray stone downtown church it seemed certain that neither the organist nor the choir would get there, much less any members of the congregation. Dr. Broyles, who lived in Ansley Park, a couple of miles away, managed to arrive — late — and one by one the organist, the choir director, the soloist, and members of the choir slipped and slid in.

Should they go on with the service? Dr. Broyles left the decision up to the choir.

Some of them lightly suggested that they should emulate the credo of the entertainment world: "The show must go on." He donned his robe and went to the pulpit. Half a dozen people had arrived.

The music started and a few more came. He said a prayer and looked up to find others tiptoeing in. The church was by no means filled, but a fair number of people got there to hear the lovely Christmas music, to lift their voices in the old carols, and to listen once more to the promise:

"Behold I bring you good tidings of great joy, which shall be to all people."

Months later Dr. Broyles had a letter from the South Pacific which alone made that morning's effort worthwhile. A soldier on his way home for Christmas Day before being shipped to the Pacific, had been stranded in Atlanta by the ice storm. He knew by daybreak that he was not going to make it home but would have to turn around and return to his outfit the minute trains and planes started traveling. He was a frustrated, lonely, angry young man, and he set out walking aimlessly around the icy streets, not the least caring how hazardous it was.

He reached Peachtree Street and North Avenue and heard music. He turned and saw candlelight beyond the church's stained-glass windows. He went in.

That Christmas service was the last he had of home and country before he was shipped to a jungle in the Pacific, he wrote, and the memory of it had stayed with him and comforted and cheered him through heat and hunger and bitter fighting. He wanted to say thank you.

The impressive thing to me is that those choir members never once considered calling off the service.

I like church people. Those who complain of pretenders and snobs and hypocrites within churches don't take into account the thousands of plain, quiet ones who literally believe that they are under a mandate to feed the hungry, clothe the naked, visit the sick, and minister unto strangers and those in prisons.

I like those like the late Miss Pauline Dennis, a retired school teacher, who rounded up slum children for Sunday school and somehow got them shoes and haircuts and campships. I like those who hold English-language classes and find homes and jobs for displaced Cubans, who conduct well-baby clinics for slum dwellers, nurseries for the children of working mothers. I like those who by their tithes and offerings support places where Alcoholics Anonymous groups and Boy and Girl Scouts are welcome to meet. I think it is lovely that they seek out strangers and say, "Come and join us," although I am aware that some people regard that as a sort of evangelical complacency. I marvel that I have never once asked a church, any church of any denomination, for help for a prisoner, a lonely old person, a homeless child, that they have not responded promptly and generously. I like church people.

These are but outer evidences of what is known as inner grace, I am sure, and I won't presume to go into grace, which Thomas Merton called "invisible and unpredictable." But I like what I know of it, regard it as perhaps not a small blessing but as the foremost blessing.

Pots and Pans

In one of Conrad Richter's books, I forget which one, there is a young pioneer woman who lives in an isolated area in the woods. Company is a rare and exciting event in her life, and when somebody comes to see her she plunges into a furious flurry of preparation. She has only one pot and it means that she has to cook one thing at the time, rushing down to the spring to scrub her vessel between each cooking. Of course she doesn't want a visitor to know she has but one pot because the inconvenience is of small moment to her and the pot itself pleases her as she scrubs it with sand and the clear, sweet spring water.

The rest of the tale has slipped from

memory in the years since I read it, but the girl and her pleasure in hospitality and her one pot come often to mind.

Kitchenware was long my pet economy. I loved pots and pans, but I always felt I could manage with what I had and it was rank extravagance when we needed so many other things to squander money on a skillet or a saucepan.

Through the years, however, in brief and fleeting seasons of affluence — when I sold a story or a book, usually — I have acquired most of the utensils I need, but I have never been able to take them for granted. I think it goes back to my childhood when the aluminum lady came to call on us.

My mother had pots and pans aplenty, but most of them were well-worn hand-me-downs from her mother-in-law's kitchen. She diligently scrubbed the cake pans to keep them bright, and when a saucepan sprang a leak there was in the cupboard drawer a little package of Mend-its so cunningly wrought even a child could plug a pot hole if necessary. (What, by the way, ever happened to Mend-its and to the practice of patching pots?)

We didn't have *new* pots until the aluminum lady came to call on us, and we didn't, of course, have aluminum. The skillets were all iron, and the boilers (we didn't call them saucepans then) were enamelware called, for some reason, "granite." There were tin pans for washing and baking, but mostly we had iron and enamelware.

The aluminum lady meant to change all that, and she sat on the porch for some time talking up the advantages of this light and strong and indestructibly shiny new metal. To dazzle my mother's eyes she opened a suitcase and set out a glorious array of boilers and bakers and frivolous egg poachers and chicken roasters in every size, all enticingly gleaming. My mother coveted the whole layout, and her fingers lovingly hefted the little saucepans, enjoying the feel of balance and pristine newness. But those were Depression years, and, as she told the aluminum lady, if we could get the rations, we had the pots to cook them in.

The aluminum lady packed up her wares

and was about to go, but there was one small saucepan that she hadn't stowed away. She held it in her hands, moving it slightly, as a hypnotist might move a bangle before his subject's eyes. Muv watched, helplessly fascinated. And then the aluminum lady stooped to stow the pot in her suitcase.

"Wait!" Muv cried, "I want that!"

She ran to get her purse. I think the saucepan may have been a sample. As I recall, it cost eighty-five cents. But it was the star of our kitchen for many years. We believed that it possessed all the magical properties that the aluminum lady had attributed to it, and when it was not in use we kept it gleaming like silver and hanging where it would show up to the best advantage over the sink.

In the years that have passed, my mother has acquired whole sets of aluminum pots and pans, and then she has given those away and bought herself complete outfits of stainless steel. She is a profligate pot buyer. I, too, have acquired enough pots — not splurgy sets, of course, but one at a time and after considerable weighty thought and soul-searching. And I love every one of them.

An electric dishwasher handles the crockery and the glasses for me, but I hand-wash the pots and pans. It's my theory that the washer doesn't clean them well, but the truth is that I like washing them. I love their copper bottoms gleaming from the iron pot rack my neighbor Harry Bailey made in his blacksmith shop and hung over my stove, and I don't mind the little extra effort it takes to scrub them with polish after each using. I like the feel of ample wooden handles, the texture of old and well-used black iron. Now and then somebody gives me a kitchen utensil. My friend Hazel Fields was inspired to buy me as a housewarming present a fluted muffin iron which I keep hanging by the stove, an ornament to all my days and occasionally a purveyor of hot bran muffins or little ruffled sweet cakes.

There's satisfaction in having a pot of just the right size when you are of a mind to make vegetable soup and to have enough cookie sheets when you are ready to make cookies. I like the shape and color of a teakettle, and blue and yellow mixing bowls please my eyes even as my hands touch their cool symmetry. I know the danger of placing too much stock in Things, but I can't help it, I feel like at least a minor Midas when I reach for and find a pot.

And sometimes I let my hand rest a moment on the now battered and not so shiny little aluminum saucepan which my mother was ready to discard years ago but handed down to me instead.

Sights

Now I don't remember how the paragraph reached my desk, but it was there, a clipping from *The Catholic Digest*, and in the nine or ten years which have elapsed since I first saw it I've been very grateful to the unknown donor.

A four-year-old child — I don't know whether boy or girl — was quoted as saying, "Stop working, Mother, and let's go outside and get some use out of the world."

It's funny how after you grow up and get busy you forget the pure delight of taking a walk, looking at the sky, wading a creek, lying on your belly in the grass making a clover chain with someone you love.

In her younger days my mother was a woman of tremendous energy and almost limitless ways of using it, and she didn't often knock off work and wander in the woods with me. But when she did it was a marvelous treat for me. Looking back, I remember all the walks we took together more vividly and with more happiness than I remember all the useful, practical, necessary things she did in the house when she was too busy to take a walk.

The scrubbed pots have long since been forgotten. The mended clothes, the let-down hems were probably of more importance then, as were the meals she cooked, the walls she painted, the garden she tended. But the times she spent just with me "getting some use out of the world" are the times I remember best.

Sometimes when we walked, plants engrossed her and we went home laden with flowers or bright-colored leaves. Sometimes she marked special little bushes, a sweet shrub or a laurel, and made plans to come back and move them to our yard. Sometimes we sat on an old wooden bridge used by the logging teams and dangled our bare feet in the water or watched entranced as a scarlet maple leaf made its way downstream through the shoals of pickerelweed and white hatpins.

Sometimes she climbed fences like the tomboy she had been in her girlhood and raced me to the next bend in the road.

Because of the words of that unknown four-year-old and the memory of my own delight in a walk with my mother I have seldom felt guilty over dropping any household chore and sallying forth with my children and grandchildren. And great is the reward.

As Rachel Carson wrote in her lovely posthumously published book, *The Sense of Wonder,* children, probably because they are small themselves, are more likely to see the "world of little things," the parts instead of just the whole. Grownups see the shape and color of the day, the hulk of that gray rock, the pattern of that stand of young pines against the sky. Children drop to their knees with sounds of excitement and discovery and pick mirrorlike fragments of mica out of the earth. They see stones shaped like wondrous birds and beasts, they note that the gray rock is starred with tiny lichens in designs very like green snowflakes. A single sassafras leaf, shaped like a mitten and colored Christmas red, pleases them as much as a forest full of brilliant leaves.

A snail on a rosebush in the yard is a great nuisance to me, and I have plotted to trap the slimy slugs which infest baby seedlings in the greenhouse. But a child watching the damp trail of silver one of these creatures makes across a leaf or a stone is caught up in the wonder of his life.

The white-veined leaf of a diminutive pipsissewa in the pine woods attracts the child, the stand of bracken on the hill is a rain forest to him. The day sky in all its changeable moods engrosses him and if, forgetting bathtime and bedtime, you go out with him and look at the night sky you have seats to an extravaganza. As Miss Carson pointed out, if the "misty river of the milky way, the patterns of the constellations standing out bright and clear, a blazing planet low on the horizon" were to be seen only once in a century we would throng out in great crowds to look at them. But because we can see them almost any night we end up not looking at them at all.

Maybe the best thing about these small

voyages of discovery with the children is what the sharing builds between us. Our boy Charles, called Bird, was seven or eight and had been out exploring by himself many times, but after one of our walks together he invited me, with an air of mystery, to come and see his "Place." His own, his special place, was a secret enclosure of green so close to the house and our road that I should have seen it. But I hadn't and I was overwhelmed when he pushed back a curtain of muscadine vines and made me welcome to a mossy hillock by a sandy ditch, where a little rain water stood and ferns and bluets grew.

There was a tree for climbing and a thick wild grape vine for swinging. He waved me to the loop the vine made for a seat and placed himself on the lowest branch of the tree, convenient for talking.

"Do you like it?" he asked.

"Like it?" I said chokily. "I love it. It's the finest 'Place' I ever saw."

It still is because of the memory of the day and the little blond boy perched on the bough over my head like a goldfinch and the honor he had bestowed on me.

Smells

Once I was in an automobile accident which hurled me into the shattered windshield. Even as they hauled me to the hospital with blood from cuts across my nose and cheeks and hands spurting all over the Good Samaritan's upholstery, I remember howling about one thing only — my eyes. I had glass in my eyes. The disfiguring slashes across my face didn't bother me in the slightest. They might even improve my appearance, I thought. But to have my eyesight endangered terrified me.

As it turned out an eye specialist awaited me in the emergency room and he painstakingly picked out the fragments of glass and my vision wasn't even threatened. I have been glad about that nearly every day since.

But one of the senses which isn't celebrated as often and as fervently is the sense of smell. I love smells but I wouldn't have thought to recognize this for the gift it is until my brother-in-law told me one day that he is anosmic, his olfactory apparatus had never developed.

"You can't smell gingerbread baking?" I cried out in pity and disbelief.

He shook his head. "Neither good smells nor bad smells," he said cheerfully.

I have thought of him and what he is good humoredly missing almost daily since. On the coast once a lady told me that she was saved from death by snakebite because she smelled a cottonmouth moccasin coiled up on her porch in time to avoid stepping on him.

"*Smelled* him?" I repeated, astonished. "Cottonmouths were near neighbors to us in the swamps and piney woods of south Alabama, but I don't remember ever noticing that they had B.O."

"They have," she said. "A nasty smell — like rotten watermelon."

Except when people have smelled smoke in time to escape burning to death I don't know of any other instances when a sense of smell has saved a life. But I know of plenty of occasions when it has enhanced a life. Mine.

The smell of sun on pine trees is the scent of security to me because the safe and warm home of my childhood was in the pine woods. Bananas are the smell of plenty — something good to eat in the house. The sharp, nose-stinging fragrance of orange peel, even in today's acceptance of oranges as an everyday staple, reminds me of Christmas. The subtle blend of creek water, pond algae, wet wood, and wool drying in the sun takes me back to the summer afternoons of my childhood when I spent every possible moment in or around the millpond.

For most of us scent borne on a random breeze unlocks recollection. Margaret Mitchell, the delightful little woman who wrote *Gone with the Wind,* once told me that when she went to Boston to be feted on the publication of her book, the celebration was nearly ruined for her because her hosts kept sending her corsages of gardenias. She could not tell them, she said ruefully, that the heavy sweet fragrance of these flowers was not festive but funereal to her because the flowers, which we call cape jessamine, were the number-one funeral flower in the South. (Neither did Miss Mitchell tell her hosts that the song which they played when she entered a room — "Marching Through Georgia" — was not the state song but the fearful paean of death and destruction played by the South's most hated enemy, William Tecumseh Sherman.)

They meant well, her hosts did, and Peggy Mitchell was raised too nice to enlighten them.

Having come along somewhat later than Miss Mitchell, I do not associate gardenias with funerals. Store-bought carnations had come into vogue by the time I went to my first funeral, and I didn't like them for the same reason that Peggy Mitchell didn't like gardenias. To me gardenias are neither funeral flowers nor party flowers, but they do have a holiday association. They came into bloom in the dooryards throughout south Alabama about the time school ended for the summer, and I associate their cloying sweetness with hot schoolrooms, the departure of the teacher we usually never saw again, barefoot weather, and impending freedom. Is it any wonder that I coddle four gardenia bushes in my yard and yearn for more?

Somewhere Montaigne suggested that physicians might use odors more often in the cure of their patients because of their ability to change and move spirits and "work strange effects" on people. He pointed out that the use of incense in churches had "rejoyced," comforted, quickened, roused, and purified the senses "so that we might be the apter and readier unto contemplation."

Montaigne may have had a good idea except for the fact that one person's "rejoyceful" smell may be like gardenias to Margaret Mitchell, an anathema to somebody else. I am not partial to on-purpose fragrances. The smell of incense in a church can be like the perfume on another woman in a closed car on a rainy day — heavy and headachy.

The light whiff is the thing, and I have found that on a frosty winter morning when you cross a skunk's trail on the road the acrid scent he left in the air is not altogether unpleasant. This will, I know, get me argument from anybody who has had too much skunk too close, but that's not what I'm talking about. I'm talking about a *little* of the musk, a trace of it in the crisp, fresh air.

The smell of grease is unpleasant, but that of frying bacon an enticement. The degree and the stage have much to do with it. I was amused to read in an old book that E. A. Bowles, a dedicated gardener, found many of the smells in his domain unpleasant. He thought phloxes smelled like a pigsty, the lusty flowering hawthorne was redolent of dead fish, and some of the brooms, which I covet for my yard, he said smelled like a dirty, soapy bath sponge.

Not to me.

Some weeds are offensive, Jimson weed especially. And ligustrum is one shrub which, to me, doesn't deserve yard room anywhere because of the stench of its blossoms in the spring. The other privets are almost as stinky, but then they are seldom planted anymore, since the yardmen it takes to keep them trimmed and shaped now have other fish to fry.

Almost everything else that grows smells good to me — hayfields, hemlock forests, geraniums and violets and roses, horse mint by the roadside and wild plums and blackberries, goldenrod and sourwood, fox grapes and ripening persimmons. I have tried for years to have a small white fragrance garden in the area where my two cabins make an ell. Gradually I have planted things that have sweet-scented white flowers. It is by no means finished, but every step of it has been fun — acquiring a Cherokee rose to plant by the corner of the cabin to hide an ugly plastic stack pipe from the bathroom, for instance.

The Cherokee rose is Georgia's state flower. Remembering it from my childhood, when it grew profligately in south Alabama, climbing trees and covering sheds and filling the air with its fresh, pure fragrance, I thought it would be easy to acquire a plant.

No nursery seems to stock this wild rose. Indeed, in some parts of the state it has been regarded as a rampant nuisance and eradicated so thoroughly that many Georgians no longer remember what the Cherokee looks like. I launched a search and happily a legislator from a county near the coast — Representative Paul Nessmith of Statesboro — recognized the Cherokee in his woods and dug up some plants and brought them to me.

In early spring when little else blooms my Cherokee with its lacy, near-thornless foliage strings open, golden-hearted single roses up the gray log walls of my cabin, offering its perfume only to those who draw close and seek it.

Because the sense of smell is memoristic, I wanted in my little plot all the fragrances of my youth of course. Two of these, still to be tested by north Georgia weather, are the tea olive (osmanthus, also called sweet olive) and the banana shrub. The tea olive has leathery, dark leaves, very like a holly, but its clusters of small creamy blossoms, which show up in February in my mother's garden and again in the fall, are its reason for being. I can believe that its fragrance, which is more subtle than magnolia but almost as pervasive, had a lot to do with setting the scene for the glamorous goings on in old Rita Hayworth movies because the tea olive originated in Asia.

The banana shrub also thrived in south Alabama — a member of the magnolia family with creamy little magnolia-shaped blossoms of unsurpassed fragrance. We used to tie these tiny blossoms in our handkerchiefs and take them to school to perfume our pockets and our desks, not for just one day but until they shriveled or fell apart.

These sweet smellers may not survive in north Georgia, where subfreezing temperatures frequently hit us. Neither may the gardenias nor, for that matter, the white azaleas and camellias, although they have survived several winters. If I'm down to two white violets and a bed of lilies of the valley when spring comes, I'll just start over again. Part of the pleasure in fragrant plants is that they are tender and transient — something to value ardently while you have them but not to count on.

Without flowers it would be a drab life, of course, but not devoid of fine evocative smells. I sometimes think that a large measure of my delight in the early morning hours is due to the fact that they are coffee-perfumed. Is there anything any better than the smell of fresh-made coffee? Oh, of course, there's the smell of roasting coffee and coffee being ground, but we don't do that any more. Fresh-made bread comes a close second, but that's not daily at our house either.

Nearly all cooking smells are good ones. (My friend Frances Tabor would mention an exception: chitlings. Her husband, Herbert, buys them canned and fries them up for himself and his men cronies when she is away from home, but he vows that she can smell them when she reaches the city limits and always hits the house raising windows.) I read somewhere that one of the unattractive smells of New York slums was the aroma of cabbage cooking. I happen to like cabbage and I learned that even when you boil it, you can somehow avert the bad smell by cooking it uncovered. On the other hand, there's a heaven-scented way to cook cabbage — shredded, lightly sautéed in butter in a wok, and dusted with nutmeg.

The smell of onions cooking is an inviting smell, and a good garlicky roast attracts some of us. All greens, mustard, collards, turnips, smell good to us.

Let's see what else: fat pine, wood smoke, fresh milk, new shoes, old books, new newspapers, little children, chocolate fudge, lye soap, country stores, cedar waterbuckets, clean sheets, seed bins, damp earth, candlewax, spring water, new paint, ocean breezes, ripe peaches, burning leaves, wild honey, summer rain, new mown grass, old leather . . . the list is endless.

Thank heaven.

Lagniappes

Where I grew up in Mobile, Alabama, we learned many things from our French and Creole neighbors — the proper appreciation of garlic, for example, and the joy of the lagniappe. Every child who went to the grocery store to make a sizable purchase for his mother or to pay a grocery bill of standing did so with the exciting knowledge that the grocer would give him a "'nappe."

Bold boys would sometimes demand their 'nappes. I remember my early embarrassment at hearing an older cousin demand imperiously of the grocer, "What about our 'nappes? Whatcha gon' give us for a 'nappe?"

Being a girl and shy I preserved the

fiction that the "little something extra" which constitutes a lagniappe was always a surprise, totally unexpected and altogether delightful. Sometimes it was a bitter disappointment to me — when the grocer gave you licorice, for instance, and you hated licorice.

But mostly the lagniappe was what it was meant to be — a little gift, an unsought treat, a spirit-lifter, a day-brightener.

Grocers no longer give you lagniappes, I'm afraid, but that doesn't mean that they have vanished from our civilization. They come in other ways when you least expect them, the little something extra, an unexpected note in the mail, the basket of vegetables a neighbor leaves by the back door, the little goodie you neither ordered nor earned.

There was the day I came home and found an earthenware soup pot on the back porch, for instance. I had admired one in my neighbor Duke Wolff's kitchen when I saw her boiling corn on the cob in it one night. She told me where she bought hers, but when I went to get one they were out.

"Mrs. Wolff just bought our last one," the clerk said.

So when I found it on my back porch I thought she had merely shopped for me, and I tried to reimburse her.

"It's my gift to you," she said lightly. "You can't pay. After all, it's just a soup pot, not a Jaguar or a Rolls."

Without meaning any disrespect to those fine automobiles, I'd rather have the soup pot. It's a lovely brown pot, made in Italy with the proper glaze for using on the stove and then storing in the refrigerator — plump and capacious and a fine catchall for that leftover roast and gravy, the half cup of green beans, two or three tablespoons of cold turnip greens. (I tried this and it's almost as good as the Portuguese kale soup they serve on Cape Cod at Provincetown.) It will inspire me to try those French soup recipes which run heavily — but more glamorously — to the staple fare of my childhood, dried peas and beans. I'll even try what one French soup-maker suggested, boiling onions whole and unpeeled in my soup.

The skins give the broth a nice color and, best of all, you don't have to chop 'em and weep, say the French.

Anne McFarland, who lives up the road from Atlanta in the old town of Marietta, is an inveterate clipper and mailer and the donor of what may be the best lagniappe you can have: response. To have somebody listen to what you say or read what you write and respond is somehow always a surprise to me — an enchanting, bolstering surprise.

A letter from Anne is a collection, an accumulation — clippings and notes with penciled comments all through the text and along the margins. Sometimes she jeers, sometimes she applauds, often she adds an experience or a recollection of her own. Now and then to keep me up to snuff she throws in a religious tract she has picked up somewhere like the magpie she is.

Although I am nearly always alarmed by handbill and signpost scriptural warnings, I read them faithfully, sooner or later. Those signs the zealous put along the roadside were meant for the likes of me, I'm sure, because when I careen around the rocky precipice in the north Georgia mountains at night and my headlights pick up the warning in yellow paint on a boulder, "Repent or burn in hell!" my adrenalin starts racing around and clawing at my pores. I'll never forget the week I covered a murder trial in a little mountain town and passed such a sign twice daily. No matter whether it was rainy or foggy or pitch black dark, the words leaped out at me in luminous yellow — the very color, I imagine, of sulphur and brimstone. That week I almost perfected the art of instant repentance.

When Anne McFarland throws in a scriptural scary I sometimes don't read it, tucking it into my pocketbook on the theory that I'll get to it later. One midwinter afternoon after weeks of being stuck indoors at the state capitol, covering the legislature, I got out unexpectedly early and started walking back to the office. More as an excuse to stay out in the sunshine than because I was interested in the merchandise, I strolled, looking in windows.

The air had the cool clean taste of

mountain springs, and the midwinter sky was the color of Michaelmas daisies. People who had been hurrying along with their heads bowed against the wintry wind were strolling and sniffing the air, savoring the lagniappe of a springlike day in the knowledge that they might not get another one for weeks and weeks.

Although I had work to do I thought of begonia bulbs and ducked into a seed store. There was a wheelbarrow full of leftover daffodils, and I yearned over them long moments, the thrifty side of me arguing that it was too late to plant them (see, they're sprouting already) and the fool optimist contending that they were gorgeously cheap and, who knows, they might be the eagerest bulbs you ever saw. A clerk saved me from that particular struggle by pointing out the snowdrop bulbs, marked down to a fantastic fifty for fifteen cents.

Well, you can't get fifty anythings for fifteen cents, I decided exultantly, and squandered thirty cents on two little perforated sacks full. They were stamped "Product of Holland," and I opened one

134

to sniff the earthy scent of the tiny bulbs and to hold one between my fingers, marveling at the miracle of a dull, dun-colored little tuber that was going to make me a real show of springtime bloom.

Walking slowly back to the office I even dwelled dreamily on what a lovely bond a handful of snowdrop bulbs constitutes between a woman who digs in the red earth of Georgia and some flaxen-haired Dutch lady working beside a Holland canal. The promise, the potentiality of bulbs awes me. If a warty, misshapen lump like a begonia tuber, for instance, can produce the delicate perfection of a Crimson Ballerina, it does seem that the possibilities in people would be unlimited.

That theme engrossed me happily for several blocks, and then Anne's scrap of scripture fell out of my pocketbook as I reached for something else. As I picked it up I found that for once it wasn't a warning but a benediction:

"Truly the light is sweet, and a pleasant thing it is for the eyes to behold the sun." (Ecclesiastes)

Weeds

A man on a television talk show once expressed the belief that I like weeds so much I probably qualify as their number-one local champion. Not so, unless everybody else in our five-county metropolitan area is totally indiscriminate about hating weeds. His statement that I "just love" weeds was about as accurate as that oldie, "She just *loves* people." I love *some* people and *some* weeds, not all of either.

Anybody would be a perfect idiot to profess to be crazy about creeping Charlie (also called gill-over-the-ground and ground ivy), a junior-grade version of that great strangler, kudzu. When I first came to Sweet Apple a neighbor gave me a box of plants. She also gave me — inadvertently, I hope — my start of creeping Charlie.

I should have known better from its square stem and pungent smell that it was a member of the mint family and therefore invincible. If it had been kudzu I would have recognized the danger right away. But creeping Charlie (other names: Robin-run-in-the-hedge, cat's foot, and *Glechoma hederacea*) is a small and delicate-looking plant, until it takes over, and how was I to know that if I dropped it on the ground I was done for?

Everywhere that sneaky rascal touches the earth it takes root and sends out runners in all directions, gobbling up the grass, choking the flowers, climbing over shrubs and vines, and even rushing and overwhelming the bricks of the terrace.

No, I don't like all weeds. I see no useful purpose in creeping Charlie. Even Johnson grass, which is a stubborn invader of the vegetable garden, was once regarded as a valuable pasture grass, I understand, and I can give it that, even as I wearily and futilely grub away trying to evict it.

The television interviewer had reason to believe that I am a weed buff because I do regard so many of them as interesting. I think I am disposed to like weeds for the same reason my great-grandmother learned to make so many different pies, cakes, and puddings from sweet potatoes. As my mother explained it, "Grandma had more sweet potatoes than anything else." I have more weeds than anything else.

In self-defense I have had to look closely and appreciatively at cockleburs instead of artichokes because cockleburs were *there*. I found out from an old herbal that this pesky plant is regarded as desirable in some parts of France because of its use as a tisane or tea and that old-timers dried its leaves, poured boiling water over them, and let them steep, sweetened the brew with honey, and drank it for sore throats.

I found that alder, which is a very invasive shrub, was a well-known source of dye for centuries, producing colors ranging from black to cinnamon to yellow, depending upon which part of the plant you used and whether you mixed copperas in the water. It gave a certain glamour to the plant when I learned that the city of Venice was built largely on alder pilings.

Fleabane, a tall weed with greenish white, daisylike blossoms, take the edges of my yard with no protest from me. I learned from a neighbor years ago that although its little flowers aren't particularly prepossessing in themselves, they combine with other flowers and give a charming showery effect to flower arrangements, very like baby's breath, which is much harder to grow. Besides, I never pick it without remembering the promise of one old-time herbalist that it would "helpe to cure one of the frensie."

Plantain is a weed I found hard to love because it has ugly, coarse leaves and flourishes in the most noticeable places in my yard — submerging the grass at the front steps, shouldering out the flowers in borders and beds. But then I looked it up and found that the ugly leaf seemed to the Indians to be shaped like a foot, the white man's foot, and that it appeared everywhere in this country that Europeans went. So they called it white man's foot. Shakespeare knew it and had Benvolio recommend it to Romeo as a poultice for his broken shin, and there is considerable lore to the effect that it will draw poison out of snakebites, cure diarrhea, and relieve sore eyes. How can you despise a useful weed like that?

Even the dandelion, which devotees of the flawless-lawn cult deplore and fight hip and thigh, is well regarded by the herbalists. It had real status in pharmacopoeia years ago, and a tincture from its dried roots is still sold by some pharmacists. The fact that it was a diuretic earned it the French name of *pissenlit* or "piss-in-bed." My only complaint about dandelion is that, even taking the yard as it does, there never seems to be enough to make the famous dandelion wine.

Interest in and acceptance of weeds does lead a gardener down some very pleasant avenues in reading and conversation. I have enjoyed many visits with mountain "yarb doctors," and I especially enjoyed a brief, by-mail acquaintance with the late Euell Gibbons, celebrated author of *Stalking the Wild Asparagus* and *Stalking Healthful Herbs* among other works.

Mr. Gibbons was less renowned for his verses than for his knowledge of how to convert weeds into gourmet meals. But I am the proud possessor of two of his lessons-from-the-wild poems, one written as an autograph in my copy of *Stalking the Wild Asparagus* and the other sent in a letter.

In the letter Mr. Gibbons wrote of the despised snail:

> Come listen to this little tale about the lowly, humble snail. While crawling on a rotten log he isn't putting on the dog. He doesn't think, as on he labors, that he is better than his neighbors, nor that he is a little god; he knows he's just a gastropod.
>
> Though he is host to liver flukes he doesn't merit our rebukes. He doesn't do as humans do and brag of blood that's really blue. He mentions not his family tree nor does he care for pedigree — admits his kin are slugs and whelks

and doesn't try to join the Elks.

When Cupid's bow lets fly a dart that strikes the snail's two-chambered heart, and he starts out his love to find, he doesn't seek a higher kind. He knows no name in upper crust will help him satisfy his lust, and genealogy can't prevail when he just wants another snail.

The tribute to the snail I had heretofore abhorred goes on for many stanzas before Mr. Gibbons concludes:

I look about me, see our land with junk car piles on every hand — billboards obstructing every view, a parking lot where trees once grew, pulluted air, polluted streams, eroded soil and broken dreams, a rising crime rate, crowded jails. Are humans really smart as snails?

Maybe even more expressive of Mr. Gibbons' feeling about wild things is his "To a Friend" verse penned on the flyleaf of my book:

I would not chain a falcon to my
   wrist
Nor jail a mockingbird within
   a cage.
For I can love the free and do
   not insist
That wildings be reduced to
   vassalage.
I would not tame the white-tailed
   doe, nor make
Wildflowers grow in cultivated
   ground,
They bloom not only for my
   selfish sake —
Not for my ears alone, the
   songbird's sound.
I cannot own the distant shining star
Nor yet its light is treasured none
   the less
And you are precious, being what
   you are
For I can love, and never need
   possess.
I claim you not, and still my love
   survives,
Though winds of freedom blow
   between our lives.

Mr. Gibbons did much to make the entire world aware of the beauty and usefulness of weeds — something many of my country neighbors knew of necessity all their lives. The handsome pokeweed, for instance, with its wine-dark stems and white flowers in the summer, was an important food plant in the spring. The catnip, which I give free rein in the garden, was "the saving of the settlemint" many years ago when doctors and drugstores were far away and people came down with colds and grippe, according to Mrs. Lum Crow. Its leaves, dried or fresh, made a tea that was strengthening and very efficacious in producing curative sweats.

But creeping Charlie? As far as I know there's nothing good to be said of it.

And yet, in a larger sense, we are indebted to this pest, I suppose. Not long ago I found a tall, slender plant out by the fence with small lavender blooms of great delicacy and charm. I looked it up in a wildflower book with some excitement, I confess. Imagine my disappointment to find that it was nothing but the naked-flowered tick trefoil. You guessed it — beggar's ticks.

I read the description again: "The small, roughly triangular seed pods of this common weed have hooked bristles that enable them to steal a ride of considerable distance by adhering to the clothing of people or to the hair or wool of animals."

Suddenly I remembered Loren Eiseley's lovely story *The Immense Journey,* a collection of essays about man's progress from primordial ooze to become a creature who flies in the sky and seeks out the stars. And I realized that I had by my front fence part of the miracle.

In my favorite chapter, "How Flowers Changed the World," Dr. Eiseley tells us that about a hundred million years ago flowers were not to be found anywhere on the five continents. Life on the planet was dominated by ugly reptiles and "a few lizard-like birds with carnivorous teeth." Mammals were small and unimpressive and remained in the shadow of the mighty reptiles.

Then one day in the Dinosaur age a single simple flower worked its way up and began scattering its seeds — "a profound innovation in the world of life." Animal life changed. There were juicy and enticing fruits to feed mammals, grass grew, insects arose to feed on the sources of food, descendants of the toothed lizard-bird lost their teeth and acquired beaks to peck seeds and gobble insects. Great herbivores like horses and bisons appeared, and among them carnivores like the saber-toothed tiger, which also sustained itself on nutritious grasses.

"One day a little band of . . . apes shambled out of the grass," wrote Dr. Eiseley. "The human story had begun." He concludes:

Without the gift of flowers and the infinite fruits, man and bird, if they had continued to exist at all, would be today unrecognizable. Archaeopteryx, the lizard-bird, might still be snapping at beetles on a sequoia limb; man might be a nocturnal insectivore gnawing a roach in the dark. The weight of a petal has changed the face of the world and made it ours.

Now when I pass the beggar's tick on the road I bow respectfully. In the fall I don't mind picking its stubborn little seeds of my shoestrings and sweater.

Homecoming

Homecoming must be a universal joy. By sheer accident I once saw England's Queen Elizabeth go home to Windsor Castle and, watching from the gate, it seemed to me that she paused a minute by the gray walls to look lovingly at the light on them and that there was affection in the touch of her hand as she reached out to open the door. (Prince Philip got there in time for that chore, it turned out, although for a minute I thought from the leisurely way he walked around the car and seemed to be enjoying the sunshine, he was going to let the Queen open the door for herself.)

Later, when we arrived back at the Atlanta airport and were met by all the family, I thought of the Queen and her homecoming and I knew that she doesn't have it any better than the humblest of her subjects or us commoners across the sea. If it's home and you love it, there's always magic in coming back to it.

That night at the airport my grandchildren had momentous news for me.

"'Tine, Ted can tie!" they cried.

In the confusion of greeting everybody and collecting our baggage I let that announcement go by at first. Then they set up a clamor.

"'Tine, Ted can TIE!" they shouted urgently.

"He can what?" I asked, looking at the little redhead, who clung to his father's hand, self-conscious but illumined by a new pride. He was the youngest of them then, three years old to their four and five. (He has a younger sister now.)

"He can tie, he can tie, he can tie his SHOES!" his brother and his two cousins chanted triumphantly.

"Oh, Ted!" I said, overwhelmed. I knelt down in the middle of the airport concourse and held out my arms to him.

The Queen, I thought fleetingly, would be lucky to come home to such a welcome.

Maybe part of the delight of homecoming is the pleasure in going away. Like most things in life there must be a certain balance. If you love to go, you love to come. I have always felt like Edna St. Vincent Millay in that poem about trains: "There isn't one I wouldn't take, no matter where it's going." Nor a plane nor a bus nor a road.

I long ago learned to keep a canvas suitcase packed with the essentials — underwear, pajamas, extra toothbrush, little cup-size electric water heater for that early morning coffee — just on the off chance that I might have to leave fast for somewhere — anywhere. It's easy enough to add a dress or two and a book and a bathing suit if you have the time.

Of course luggage is really a frill, an extra assurance of comfort, not absolutely essential to travel. I was amused a year or so ago by the lament of a woman I know whose daughter was going to travel all over Europe in blue jeans, without even a bra to sew a money pocket in. How would she carry her valuables, her mother wanted to know, and I wondered with her. But as a newspaper reporter I have taken many overnight trips without an overnight bag. I learned early in covering murder trials that in country courthouses where the washroom facilities were primitive, a cotton slip dried the hands better than nylon, although slick and not very absorbent, dried itself faster. So you didn't have to sit the rest of the day with soggy fabric clinging to your thighs.

Sometimes there's no time to pick up a bag or even buy another slip, especially in cases of tornadoes, floods, fires, and jailbreaks. But I have always gone willingly, even happily, and have seldom failed to find the country, foreign or domestic, interesting.

A trip down a Georgia highway after all these years still has charm for me. Sometimes I have felt sorry for the drivers of the big trucks, hurtling along the highway alone in the darkness, and rejoiced with them over the advent of the citizen's band radio which enabled them to chat with their colleagues. But when I am out there myself I think they have a certain edge on the rest of us, being abroad in the world with an awareness of land and sky and weather while we sleep.

Not long ago I spent two weeks in Germany, arriving at the Bonn airport to find my luggage had gone somewhere else. I had my typewriter, a toothbrush, a raincoat, and a sweater, and that was all for several days, but it didn't impair my pleasure in the new and different land in the slightest.

The German lady who was our guide put my aplomb about the missing luggage down to sportsmanship. She thought I was a real girl scout not to whine about sleeping in my slip and a sweater (it was cold) and offered to lend me a nightie. Fortunately, she wasn't sure of her grasp of English, especially southern United States English, and thought it was a language difference when I said lightly, "Oh, that's all right. I'm used to sleeping around in any old thing — with clothes or without."

I loved Germany, although it's probably

the only place in the world for which I have embarked with temperate-to-tepid enthusiasm. (I made the mistake of rereading Anne Frank's *The Diary of a Young Girl* a few weeks before my departure.) I felt twinges of homesickness now and then. But if you are a born homesick type and have had relapses all your life, you can expect along about twilight — what the Germans call "the blue hour" — to feel a sudden longing for people and a place of your own.

Now and then during a really extensive two weeks' tour with daily interviews of interesting people I would awaken in the night and wonder what city I was in and why. Everybody I love is thousands of miles away, I would think. Why am I here?

But of course, as the real travelers are certain to have discovered long ahead of me, people in a foreign land are not necessarily foreign. I don't know when it struck me that we all speak a common language in so many ways. In the important ways we understand one another the world over, I suppose.

I think the gardens were the first thing that made me realize this. All over Germany there are communal gardens for people who live in apartments or town houses and have not enough land of their own to use. A big field will be divided into small plots, each with its tool shed and sometimes a little shelter with chairs for resting and admiring your patch.

We were having lunch on the top floor of a big hotel and I looked out the window and saw an old man bent over setting out plants in a row in the dark earth. The curve of his back, the movement of his hands, the tilt of his head, all these were so familiar to me I thought in surprise, "Why I know him. All my life I've known him."

At the big Hamburg *Fischmarkt* it struck me again. A dark-haired, pink-cheeked child about the age of my youngest grandchild, Susy, saw a pen full of rabbits and poked out her baby hand to pat them. A baby's hand patting a little animal is the same in any language.

In stores sometimes the language difference makes a little trouble. But you see a young girl holding an evening dress up to her blue jeans and T-shirt and admiring herself in the mirror and you're at home once more.

Music, of course, is the famous universal language and Germans enjoy it so much. We went to an all-Beethoven concert in Bad Godesberg, near his home, and it was the same Beethoven which emanates from my son's record player at home. We went to see *La Bohème* at the Berlin opera, and Mimi's consumptive death moved us all alike. The sign *Vom Winde Verweht* on the theatre marquee didn't mean a thing to me until I saw the pictures of Vivien Leigh and Clark Gable and I was back in *Gone With the Wind* country again. Church bells, too, speak the same language and so do train whistles.

The brothers Grimm's story of the donkey, the dog, the cat, and the rooster who grew old and weren't wanted by their masters anymore is as familiar to us as it is to the people of Bremen, where they are folk heroes. You remember the donkey knew he was so old he was going to be destroyed, the cat mourned that his teeth "have lost their edge" and his mistress was going to have him drowned, the dog could no longer hunt and his master was going to have him destroyed, and the rooster "crowed in sorrow" because he overheard the farmer's wife planning to cut off his head and cook him for dinner. These oldsters, unloved and unwanted, set out to become traveling musicians with poignant optimism that conquered all. They stopped by a hut in the woods, overheard some robbers planning to loot the city, and lifted their voices in a hideous chorale which frightened the robbers away, saving the townspeople of Bremen. They are celebrated today with a statue on the west side of the city's ancient Gothic town hall, with a mural in an old wine cellar, and with paintings and monuments everywhere.

How can you not love a city — or a country — with so high regard for a fairy story?

But, as usual, I loved coming home. When we drove into the yard at Sweet Apple from the airport I was half asleep and numb from weariness, and I thought I only wanted to totter into the house and fall into the first bed I saw. Then the scent of honeysuckle reached out and enveloped me. I sat a minute sniffing and then I heard the mockingbird, and when I could get up enough strength to crawl out of the car I saw that the grass, new cut and dew-sweet, was dappled with moonlight.

May is a time of excitement to all who love the earth, no matter where you set your foot down on it, be it Europe or rural Georgia.

All the celebrated cathedrals of Germany, all the wonderful houses and gardens, including those in the Black Forest, had been much on my mind. But suddenly a ramshackle little log cabin sitting in a tangle of honeysuckle and moonlight, looked mighty splendid to me.

A trip of any kind has two high points — that moment of leave-taking when we are all, as the old expression has it, journey proud, and maybe best of all, coming home.

Changes

A friend dragged me by the film shop at lunchtime one day so she could pick up snapshots of her trip to Africa and show them to me. She couldn't wait to open the envelope and spread the pictures out on the restaurant table, hoping to recreate before our eyes the marvelous month she had spent on that mysterious and exciting continent.

They were good pictures. She is an able photographer. And together we examined them for some minutes before she pushed them aside and said sadly, "It's not the same, is it? Pictures are just pictures."

I knew how she felt. Like everybody, she had expected too much from photographs. They are a help to memory, but they cannot catch the moment and keep it for you, any more than stopping a clock makes time stand still.

All of us who have cameras hope the film record of a moment is going to reproduce it for us, I suppose, even a terrible photographer like me. (I have a marvelous collection of snapshots of my thumb.) But, of course, one of the great things about life is that it moves, changes, progresses. It is like the wild chicory, whch opens its blue, fringelike petals early in the cool and fragile morning hours and closes them in the heat of the day, or the old-fashioned day lilies, which are the more enchanting because you know when you look into their lemon and topaz depths today that they will be gone tomorrow.

Who would want them to last forever like those plastic flowers you see on the graves of country cemeteries?

We wouldn't value the white panicles of bloom of ash and sourwood so much in July if they were still there in November. I picked up a cicada on the garden path the other morning and held him for a moment in the palm of my hand, admiring the iridescent blue-green of his back, the gauzy efficiency of his wings. Then I set him gently down on the crooked trunk of the old peach tree, and the next time I looked he was gone. But the memory of his transient presence will stay with me.

The urge to stop time, to trap the moment and hold it like a bee caught in amber forever, is strong in all of us. It hits me especially when I am around the children. We sat on the terrace late one afternoon and I watched Bird remove himself from the circle of adults and climb to a perch in the peach tree. He was where he could hear the conversation below but stay detached from it. He was in a leafy cocoon insulated against the "run get" directions of the grownups. We couldn't see him, but we could see his foot, a slender, dirty, little boy's foot with scratched mosquito bites on the ankles and a rag on his big toe.

It seemed to me as I watched it swinging overhead that if you could keep a little boy with his bare feet in a peach tree you could stop time, hold back winter and age, and make it forever warm and fragrant and youthful summertime.

But would you want to? The essence of life is that it moves and changes. My mother in her eighties naturally feels that death can't be too far away, and she sometimes wants to turn the idea this way and that, considering its many facets.

Her talk about it, her wish to plan for it, have sometimes been painful to me despite my knowing, as Shakespeare has it, that death is "a necessary end" and "will come when it will come."

Once when my grandson Ted and I were visiting Muv she remarked that she was outliving all her friends and relatives and was bound to have a skimpy funeral so I was not to bother planning a gathering in the house.

"The children and grandchildren will be enough," she said, "and you won't have to bother with spreading out a lot of food for company."

"Look, Muv," I said, "it's too hot to plan your funeral. Let's go swimming. Want to?"

It was just what Ted had been waiting

for, of course, and Muv went and turned the burners off under the creamed corn, fried okra, pork chops, and cornbread she had started for supper. She got her bag, a cold drink, and something to read while Ted and I swam. We hurried to Round Lake and parked her in a shady spot under a big live oak tree, which drips with gray Spanish moss.

Round Lake is a pretty little body of green water with a sandy bottom. Members of Muv's family have gone there to swim as long as she can remember. Once when that part of Florida decided it was tropical enough to grow oranges there were satsuma groves around the lake, and people of Muv's generation used to catch the train from Alford, two miles away, to "go in bathing" at the lake and gather oranges.

Muv looked cheerful and lively when we came out of the water and stood around trying to drip dry a little before the trip back to the house. But she evidently was still thinking of death.

"I want you all to keep my house just as a place to come on vacations," she said. "You all love the lake and it would be so handy."

"Muv," I said, exasperated, "if you're not here it wouldn't be any fun to come here for vacations."

"Pshaw," she said. "The lake will be here and you can just pretend it's me."

It was such a fanciful idea, the lake as a stand-in for Muv, that I thought about it for a long time. Of course the lake is not Muv, but it is a pleasant representative and all of us could do worse than to pick such substitutes for the time when we have, in Muv's euphemistic phrase, "gone on."

If my children and grandchildren would look at a stream or a mountain slope and see me, instead of tying me to some tacky and dated old photograph, it would be lovely. No faults, no frailties, just beauty and strength I never had. Unfortunately, it doesn't work that way, but the idea somehow has freed me to talk of death with Muv any time she feels the need to. It may be, as she once said, the brightest wagon in the Mardi Gras parade.

Baskets

My friend Jo Severinghaus gave me a collection of small nested boxes one Christmas with a note quoting Winnie-the-Pooh that it was "something to put things in."

It wasn't the first time Jo had recognized and supplied that need for me. I always need something to put something in, and once Jo arrived with the best "something" of all, a marvelous capacious old tote basket which had belonged to her late mother. I think she brought a pie in it, but after the pie was eaten it came to hold my knitting, books to read on the bus, a pair of dry shoes for suddenly rainy days, and even an occasional sandwich. I seldom go anywhere without that basket, and when I do I regret it.

Collections, I contend, are a nuisance, taking up space which is scarce in my log cabin, and accumulating dust, which isn't. You should not, I insist, have things you don't use.

Baskets are the exception. I have so many baskets I can't possibly use them all all the time — and I love every one of them and want more. A good basket, a handmade basket, is a personal thing, as personal and well used as a dog-eared, mangled, and coverless little address book in my purse. (How do people make all those editorial decisions necessary to move into a new address book, I wonder. I can't bear to eliminate even the names of people now dead or friends I haven't seen in twenty-five years. You never know, I always say. I even retain, for heaven knows what reason, the number of the Kansas City motel where my son-in-law once stayed for a week while playing the trumpet at a nearby night spot.)

One of my most valued neighbors is Mister Jim Taylor, the basket man. His son, Wilburn, is a country fiddler, and his daughter-in-law, Ruth, is a guitar player. Mister Jim lives across the river, farming a small patch and making split-white-oak baskets when he can, as he puts it, "get the timber." White oak suitable for baskets is not as plentiful as it once was and Mister Jim, now in his eighties, isn't up to wandering too far afield to search.

His baskets are beautiful because they are so sturdy and functional. Once some city visitor asked him to copy a fancy-shaped machine-made basket to hold flowers, and he looked at it with some interest before he declined. The machine-made basket seemed a flimsy and frivolous thing to him and the purpose, holding flowers, was hardly worth his time. Mister Jim learned to make baskets when there were no other light and portable containers around the farm. Except for crocks and iron pots, there was hardly anything to hold anything. He made baskets for cotton pickers, baskets for bringing in beans and corn and tomatoes, egg baskets and clothes baskets. Almost every barn in the area was ornamented with Mister Jim's white-oak baskets hanging from pegs handy for hauling feed and holding kindling.

They are fragrant, white-gold in color when they are new, and they age beautifully, silvering with time and use.

Aunt Nancy Pankey, an intrepid old mountain woman I was fortunate to know before her death, told how baskets helped to keep her family alive when she was a young widow with a house full of children to feed. Her husband, a Confederate veteran, died and left Aunt Nancy with nothing but a few mountain acres and the house where they lived. She farmed singlehandedly until the children were big enough to help her, and her only source of cash was baskets.

"I'd come weakling in from the field," she once told me, "and drink a little water sweetened with syrup and go back and work till dusk-dark caught me. Then I'd set up late making honeysuckle baskets for the young'uns to sell around Ellijay square the next day. They'd get twenty-five cents apiece for them."

Now I don't have one of Aunt Nancy's

baskets. I wish I did have. But an artsy-craftsy friend of mind is pledged to make me a honeysuckle basket someday. She thinks Aunt Nancy and I have much in common because the old lady once said, "Oh, I've had a pilgrim time, I have."

When I was a child baskets made from pine needles were a specialty with everybody who went to camp or vacation Bible school. Hunks of pine needles were bound together with raffia, and many mother, mine included, had a lopsided sewing basket with an ill-fitting lid topped with a tiny pine cone for a handle. I have a much better pine-needle basket made for me by Ruth Sefton, a retired snake charmer who was my friend for many years before her death. Although she had only half her fingers on one hand, due to a rattlesnake bite in her beginning years with the carnival, she was very dexterous, making not only baskets but minute doll furniture and toys as well.

Baskets have become fashionable — and expensive — in recent years and I don't share Mister Jim's opinion of the fancy and the machine-made. To me any basket is something to covet and to use — sooner or later. I especially enjoy arranging flowers in baskets. Summer bouquets of Queen Anne's lace and daisies seem to have an affinity for old split-oak egg baskets. I once had a child's small-sized cotton-picking basket which held kindling by the hearth in winter and magnolia leaves and pine in the summer. It had a hole in the bottom which a cleaning woman seemed to think rendered it useless and she threw it out. (My howls of loss may still be heard in the land.) But if you aren't lucky enough to have an old basket of the right size a new one isn't bad. I have even set those little vegetable baskets you can get at the market for thirty or forty cents around the terrace, filling them with flowers centered by candles for night parties in the summertime.

One of my favorite machine-made baskets is an old one which my mother passed on to me as her Aunt Babe's egg basket. Aunt Babe must have had more chickens than I remember because it is a big basket — so big we use it for picnics, gathering apples, and sometimes for shopping. (I've always been sorry that the conservationists' pitch to get us all to take our shopping bags and baskets to the store didn't catch on. It seems to make salespeople nervous to have you bring your own container, as if it were a shoplifting device.)

A Cherokee princess brought me a small shallow reed basket from a North Carolina Indian reservation which I use to hold extra bars of soap in the bathroom. I have baskets to hold quilt scraps and knitting wool and garden seed and one dear-to-my-heart basket for trowels and gardening gloves. (Friends gave me a plastic container with partitions designed for this purpose. It was bright red, weatherproof, and easy to spot in the yard. I couldn't think of a single logical reason for going back to my old basket until I left the plastic garden caddy out in the rain one night and found everything in it afloat the next morning. A basket of course, would have let the water through, and when the sun came up the things it contained would dry. Reason enough for returning me to the weathered old grape basket of yore. I gave the slick new plastic garden caddy to my daughter Susan, who thinks that sometimes there's nothing more functional than plastic.)

Baskets make light and strong carrying containers for so many things. When my children were small we always had a basket bassinet for travel. I once got a big shallow flat-bottomed clothes basket for a baby who was born in jail and had been sharing an iron bunk with his mother. One day when I was not at home my prize (from the Goodwill) hamper which I kept outside the bathroom for dirty clothes turned out to be just the thing my son needed for delivering a litter of puppies to the Humane Society. He thought what the puppies did to it made it not worth bringing home, and when I called the Humane Society in an effort to reclaim it I learned that a young man who worked there had scrubbed it, painted it white, and was using it in his apartment to hold plants. The empty space where that particular basket was still haunts me.

For years I used baskets to hold my

clothes when I traveled. Some of my colleagues still remember that I went to the Georgia coast to cover the seven-million-dollar divorce trial of the late R. J. Reynolds, the tobacco tycoon, carrying a couple of changes of underwear and a dress or two in an old picnic basket. Mrs. Reynolds, they pointed out joyfully, had two wardrobe trunks and many locked cases full of jewels from Cartier and Tiffany's for the same little courthouse sojourn.

It wasn't for that reason that I gave up using baskets for baggage. If I had had trunks and jewelry cases I couldn't have filled them. But baskets have personalities of their own and I don't think they like to be used as suitcases. I have had them pop open and spill stuff many times, but when one I especially admired split its sides and spewed its contents in front of President and Mrs. Lyndon Johnson in the airport in New Orleans I switched to canvas. Not that the President or his lady noticed or cared. I had been traveling all week on the Lady Bird Special train, and I firmly believe that the then First Lady was good-humored, poised, and well able to rise above such minor crises.

I simply couldn't stand the loss of one of my favorite baskets, and there are apparently some things these charming "somethings" don't want put in them.

Understanding

One of the most satisfying blessings anybody ever had is an eye to catch — somebody across the room who sees the humor or the pathos or the absurdity or the grandeur of what is happening at the exact instant you see it and flashes you a look of appreciation and sharing.

When my child Susan was only three years old I found that quality in her, and I think it is still the thing I value most in her. If her baby sister was funny or fractious I could look up from trying to cope and find Susan's gray-violet eyes had assessed the situation and were sending me a signal of amusement or sympathy. If her older brother was obstreperous or little-boy touching, Susan saw it and telegraphed a reaction so like mine I often laughed aloud in delight and disbelief. From such a little girl such immediate rapport was a most felicitous gift.

There have been other people in life with whom I have had bonds of affection, of mutual interest or wordless communication, and without them it would have been a lonely road to travel. But sometimes the eye to catch is on a stranger.

Not long ago I was at a dinner party, seated next to a man of brilliance and great ability. The trouble is that he thinks so too, and as he talked to me earnestly and tediously of his oft-unappreciated gifts I felt utterly marooned with his ego until I looked up and saw the man across the table was listening. He caught my eye with a look so full of amusement, so cognizant of the absurdity of this long-winded genius, that I relaxed and began to enjoy the preposterous monologue. We didn't get together later for a "Did you hear him . . . ?" "Can you believe?" session, but it was almost as good as if we had.

For a little while we had been together in our evaluation of it and our amusement.

Sometimes it is the key word to an old joke that sparks the light in the eye across the way and causes it to send you a signal. Sometimes it is a mutual experience.

My mother was telling my friend Julia and me about a neighbor of hers, an elderly widow now dead, who had very surprisingly eloped with a man in a mobile home toward the end of her life.

Muv had had the temerity to ask the obvious question nobody else would ask: "Why?"

"Well, I'll tell you," the aged bride said; "I always did want to marry a man who could pray in public."

It turned out badly. The silver-tongued bridegroom wearied of his bride in a few days and in a couple of weeks she returned to her home, explaining that he had taken to locking the door against her and it had grown monotonous having to climb in through the mobile-home windows all the time.

Julia and I laughed when Muv told the

story and that was all right, but later we happened to be at a gathering where a man was asked to open the meeting with a prayer. He obliged, going along for about ten minutes, praying with feeling and obvious proficiency. I cracked my closed eyes and saw Julia's eyes were open and her shoulders were shaking with silent laughter. I had to have a coughing fit and get out of the room fast or I would have laughed aloud. Not at the man or his prayer but at the recollection of the poor widow who had always wanted to marry a man who could pray in public. I knew Julia was thinking the same thing — that here was a good candidate for her and one that might not lock her out.

The fun of an eye to catch, the sense of compatibility, of sharing, of momentary oneness, is important in what is for everybody the essentially lonely business of living. City editors and reporters are seldom totally congenial, although sooner or later most of them become fast friends. Their one reliable bond is that both city editor and reporter value a big story, a good story. But it is a rare city editor who is properly appreciative of the subtle nuances, the incongruities, sometimes the salacious details too risqué for a family newspaper, and when a reporter finds such a one it enhances the job in the field a hundredfold. Bill Shipp, now *The Constitution's* associate editor, was such a city editor.

In covering politics or a murder trial I often used to dictate a few details I knew would never see print simply because I knew Bill would enjoy them and they would increase his understanding and appreciation of what was going on at the scene. Occasionally such a line would make the paper, but what really cheered me out there in a strange town was Bill's whoop of surprise or enjoyment at the other end of the telephone.

Equally important, of course, is the flash of understanding, the bright gleam of support when it seems that what you are saying will outrage and infuriate everybody else or simply fall with a dull thud, warranting no reaction.

Sometimes understanding seems slow to come, and then some apparently insignificant thing will trigger it. It has nothing to do with an eye to catch, but sometimes I think of the rainy winter day when I suddenly understood a woman who came into our newsroom looking for help. She had a dreary little story, identical with so many others at the time, and there wasn't much we could do to help. I heard her out. She was a woman in her forties, newly divorced and trying to rear two children on the salary of a waitress, the first job she could get after years of being a stay-at-home housewife. Her teenage daughter was rebellious and difficult, but the mother had thought that things were going to be all right when the girl and her boy friend suddenly disappeared.

I wrote down the information and made the standard, she'll-show-up noises and advised her to keep checking with the police, to whom she had already made a missing-persons report, and I was walking her to the elevator when she suddenly fainted.

Somebody ran for water and a couple

of the men came over with the idea of lifting her up and taking her to the clinic. I squatted on the floor beside her and burst into tears. I had just seen where muddy water had spattered on the backs of her cheap and wrinkled old stockings. I spatter my stockings like that when I walk in the rain, and all at once the exposed weakness of that woman and my kinship to her were more than I could take. She had tried so hard, making herself as neat as possible, putting on lipstick and a bright scarf out of pride and independence. But the muddy water marks on the backs of her legs as she lay there on the floor were symbols to me of her vulnerability and loneliness and inability to handle the things that were happening to her.

I'd like to say that we met and conquered her problems for her. We did find the daughter and she came back home, and I'm not sure if things were better or worse.

Not long ago a friend who had been on the staff and present in the newsroom at the time recalled that occasion and said curiously, "You're supposed to be tough.

What happened to you that day?"

I fumbled for an explanation and then I said shamefacedly, "It took a while but . . . well, I guess I *understood*."

Sticks and Stones

Members of our family, my mother has often remarked, have never minded making fools of themselves. It's a good thing, too, because if we did we'd spend great portions of our lives in embarrassment and distress.

The minute you are born, I sometimes think, you start getting caught up in ridiculous situations. And it gets worse as you get older. When your children come along you find yourself in roles you never dreamed of assuming. I first noticed that more than twenty-five years ago when I went to my first day-camp closing exercise and the leader said, "Will the mothers of the Black Panthers please stand?"

I hadn't known I was the mother of a

black panther — even in that day before the animal took on another aura. But there I was standing, beaming at my redheaded, freckle-faced child, who was clearly — but didn't look it — a member of that sleek and dangerous cat tribe.

All mothers know that housebreaking puppies is woman's work, no matter who owns the dog. But not all mothers become town characters as a result of that chore. I did. It was when we had a cocker spaniel named Crowe for our doctor, William R. Crowe, who gave him to us. One rainy night it became obvious that Crowe needed to go outside and, as usual, nobody else was available and I was elected.

We lived in town then, and most of our yard was visible from the street. So I had to dress — in a manner of speaking. I threw a raincoat on over my pajamas, pulled on somebody's cowboy boots left by the sofa, and cast about for something to cover my head. My eye lit on a velvet picture hat one of my daughters had acquired for a school play months before. Perfect, I thought. Broad enough to keep the rain out of my face and shelter my shoulders. I put it on, grabbed up Crowe, and went outdoors.

Crowe was small and night-colored, and in the rain visibility for me wasn't too good. So I found myself wandering around under the street light, water dripping off my picture hat and falling into my cowboy boots, croaking anxiously, "Crowe! Crowe!"

I guess visibility was excellent for a young couple passing on the sidewalk. I heard them laugh, and then I heard her say, "A real eccentric. The witch of Thirteenth Street."

It doesn't improve as you get older. I undertook to deliver a handsome old iron bed to my daughter's apartment the day she was expected home from the hospital after giving birth to her second baby, Ted. That was before we had acquired a proper, suitable-for-hauling truck, and I hauled everything in my Volkswagon bug. I wasn't prepared for the sensation I would create driving down Peachtree Street with the car surrounded and enmeshed in bed.

A workman yelled, "Why don't you drive the bed and haul the car, lady?"

A policeman looked at the ornate loops and finials hanging over the windshield and called, "Where's the parade?"

And a jaunty old fellow striding along in a red jacket and brandishing a walking stick got my attention as we both stopped for a traffic light. He looked at the bed, winked at me, and said racily, "You can bring it over to my house, honey."

When we had two donkeys, Jack and Jenny, for the children I seemed to be constantly ridiculous. Donkeys are comic animals in themselves, and these two were always breaking out of the pasture and involving me in their silly charades. Early one winter morning I sailed around the house trying to get it ready for some clergymen friends of a friend who were going to swing by my cabin for morning coffee on their way to a church conference.

I had built a fire, polished the spoons, set out the good cups, measured the coffee, and was ready to get dressed in the

English-country-lady tweed skirt, cashmere sweater, and pearls I had in mind for the occasion. At that moment a neighbor called to tell me that the donkeys were strolling down the highway in greatest jeopardy. The fuel-oil man had narrowly missed bashing his truck against their ornery hides.

I threw on an army jacket over my pajamas and housecoat, put on my straw sunhat (a durable, weather-turning headpiece) stepped into some rubber wading boots I found by the backdoor, and leaped into the car and took off.

Naturally, I couldn't budge Jack and Jenny with the car. I had to get out, put halters on them and tow them bodily down the highway. Wouldn't you know the clergymen would catch me thus arrayed, sweating and tugging and cursing and calling all kinds of imprecations on the head of two balky donkeys when they arrived at Sweet Apple?

Most of the fool situations you find yourself in are child-induced, of course. You see a woman crawling around on her belly in a straw hut the size of a gopher hole and you can be sure she has grandchildren who built it and insist that she inspect it. Once I was caught in downtown traffic with only a buttonless duster covering my slip and nothing covering my bare feet.

My son and his friend had urgent, last-minute need of a ride to the ballpark and were too young to drive. I didn't think there was time to dress so I jumped in the car as-was. Naturally after I got them there and turned homeward the car choked down at a railroad crossing and no amount of tromping on the starter would get it going.

I always will feel grateful to the unidentified woman who made her husband stop and help me, when they couldn't do anything for laughing.

"There but for the grace . . ." she cried, looking at the ragged duster I clutched around my middle and my bare feet. "I've always known it was going to happen to me someday. I have children, too."

One child-induced spectacle hit me in morning rush-hour traffic downtown. Ted had been to the country for his birthday and had mistakenly left behind one of his favorite presents, a new football. He called begging me to bring it when I came to the office. His mother would meet me and pick it up.

I hadn't thought how it looked, an aging lady with gray in her hair, standing on the street corner with a football tucked under her arm like Joe Namath until somebody in a passing car pointed and laughed.

That's when the birthday present diabolically came to life, slipping from my grasp and leaping into the street. I guess I enlived work-bound traffic for a lot of people that morning, a plumpish grandmother type running and bending and swerving and ducking between onrushing vehicles in pursuit of a football. All without helmet or shin guards too.

To be impervious to ridicule may not be a blessing but not to mind it too much seems to help.

The Weather

Harry Golden, the North Carolina sage and author of such bestsellers as *For 2ᶜ Plain* and *Enjoy, Enjoy,* once suggested as a cure for lonesomeness owning a thermometer. Such a possession, said Mr. Golden, will keep you so busy checking the temperature and going back and rechecking it, studying the weather forecasts, and watching the television weather programs that, presumably, you won't have time for feeling lonesome and alone.

As usual, Mr. Golden had hold of a good idea. People who consider talking about the weather as the ultimate example of trivial and boring conversation have always astonished me. We who were brought up in the country or who live there now all know that there is nothing more vital than weather. It spells life or death to crops, it's the difference between fish biting or not biting, butchering time or not, whether the clothes will dry, the roof leak, or the firewood hold out. It's not only important, we think it is *interesting.*

Part of my enthusiasm for weather stems from the fact that I was born and grew up in that finishing school for tropical hurricanes, the Gulf Coast. From September through November we observed the weather with the most intense interest, knowing that small-craft-warning flags flying from the pole on top of the Van Antwerp building (in those days) could give way to hurricane warnings and that a hot fall day could turn stormy at a moment's notice. And they weren't piddling poetry and picturebook storms either but monstrous destroyers of property and lives at worst and one-day school closers at best.

Oh, we had a healthy respect for weather where I lived. I don't know what lore inland children are reared on, but we Gulf Coast children were nurtured on storm lore — the big tidal wave that came in at Bayou La Batre one sunny fall day and swept away a whole excursion train full of people, the 1906 storm when the water was so high they had to take old Mrs. Williams out of her attic by rowboat, the 1916 storm which took the roof off the turpentine still, the 1926 storm when live oak trees your grandpa planted fifty years ago were ripped from the earth and up-ended like matchsticks. In those days the really bad hurricanes were expected in years that had six in them. Some time in the 1930s they got off schedule. Some people blamed it on Franklin D. Roosevelt, who had the nerve to change the date of Thanksgiving and might have just been presumptuous and powerful enough to tamper with hurricanes. Then the atom bomb was dropped and it played fast and loose with all nature for a time. The last I heard from an old sea captain who professed to abhor females, more than storms, if possible, was that naming hurricanes for women did it. Women have no sense of timing, he contended, so how can you expect a storm named Camille, for instance, to stick to a schedule?

When we didn't have the storms to talk about we had the heat. It was considerable in Mobile, and although nobody expected to be really comfortable there was an elaborate set of stratagems for trying. Those who could afford it moved over the bay to Point Clear for the summer. Those who had to stay at home took up carpets, swathed the furniture in white osnaburg slipcovers and closed the blinds against the noonday sun. Young people went sailing or swimming in the bay or in the cold, clear water at the Spring Hill pumping station. And, of course, it being the 1930s, everybody spent as much time as possible in that great Arabian Nights cave of cold air and cinematic glamour, the Saenger Theater, the first air-conditioned building in town.

In between we talked about the weather — how hot it had been, how it compared to other hot days, and what the prediction was. Boring conversation? We found it endlessly fascinating.

As soon as the heat passed we settled down to alternately enjoy the winter weather and worry about its passing in time for Mardi Gras and the town's biggest tourist attraction, the opening of the azalea trail. Would the cold hold back the glorious rush of "Pride of Mobile" pink, or would it warm up so fast that the azaleas would bloom themselves out before the planned festivities?

The weather was eternally suspenseful, urgently important, and indestructibly interesting in those days, and I guess it still is to me. I count it a blessing to live in a part of the country where we have all kinds of weather, fast-changing, capricious, infinitely varied weather. An otherwise bright and intelligent young newspaperman who came from Miami to work on the Atlanta *Constitution*, alarmed me about his taste and judgment when he confessed that he missed Miami's weather.

"You *couldn't!*" I cried. "All that sunshine, all those flowers monotonously blooming all the year round! What would you do for sleet?''

At that point he made it clear that he hoped to have as little to do with sleet as possible. But I think he might change his mind. We have monstrously fine sleet on some winter nights. Not often, not regularly, just enough to make its staccato thrumming on the roof musical, just enough to sting your face with icy silver projectiles when you venture outdoors and make you glad when you can seek shelter.

Mr. Golden didn't need to tell me what a companion, what an occupation really, a thermometer can be. I have them all over the place — in the kitchen window, in the living-room window, on the back porch, and in the greenhouse. The first thing I do on arising in the morning is to start coffee and check the thermometers. It gives me matchless satisfaction to be able to report that it was an arctic eighteen degrees or a my-goodness-like-spring fifty-two degrees on a winter dawn. The rain gauge on a post in the backyard is a similar satisfaction. Loose-talking weather observers with their lazy metaphors can say it rained cats and dogs if they want to, but I glory in the precision of "Would you believe, FOUR inches in less than eight hours?"

It's not that we need thunder and lightning to appreciate the sunshine, as fair-weather addicts will sometimes suggest. Who's to say which is better? Some of us are so contrarily constructed that our spirits rise as the barometer falls. It's the variety, the unexpectedness, the never-the-sameness that makes watching and *feeling* weather rewarding enjoyment on any day of the year.

Money

Money is a blessing which has received bad press for generations. I am not one of its detractors. I think money can be lovely. I admire so many of the things it can buy — shoes for children, braces for teeth, a roof against the rain, trips and tires and apples trees.

There is a danger of overestimating its value, I suppose, and I sometimes think my country neighbors are the only people I know who have the proper focus on money. They can take it or leave it.

In the still-rural area where I live, now slowly and inexorably going suburban, there is a cadre of old country families who came down from the mountains generations ago and settled in north

Fulton County to farm for a living. They raised what they ate, and when cash money was needed most of them did what their independent Scottish forebears in the Appalachian hills had long considered an inalienable right. They went back to the branch heads and made a little moonshine.

It was a precarious enterprise. Occasionally somebody was shot at, and now and then a good, otherwise law-abiding husband and father landed in jail. But I guess it brought a certain ebullience, a joie de vivre to what would have otherwise been a grinding, spirit-breaking cycle of hard labor and frugality. For my country neighbors are joyful people, pickers, singers, buck-dancers, cooks who can turn a hoecake of cornbread and a pot of beans into a party, farmers who will not hesitate to drop the plow and pick up a fishing pole if the spring weather is right and the creek bank calls.

When I first moved to the country I had trouble sorting out what could be paid for and what couldn't. I still have a little trouble with it. We needed carpenters, electricians, plumbers, and they came and properly accepted money for their services. We needed tractor work in the yard and the garden plowed. That could be hired.

But I got the car stuck in the mud and when my neighbor Clarence brought his tractor and chains and pulled me out he was offended that I suggested paying him. His mother-in-law, Mrs. Lum Crow, had some prize boxwoods she raised from twigs, which she offered to sell me. (I didn't buy because I already had boxwood.) But she indignantly turned down pay for a bushel full of cuttings and bulbs and a side order of fried apple pies which she had for me.

Her late daughter, Olivia, our closest neighbor and friend, would accept pay for helping me with housecleaning and then give me its worth in vegetables from her garden. I could pay her to babysit with my grandchildren, but when my mother was ill and she came and did for her she was outraged by my offer of money. She would charge by the hour for dusting and mopping but bring the makings and spend a whole day helping me put up pepper relish and become angry if I reached for my pocketbook.

I am gradually learning, not by logic but by instinct, to tell the difference between hired work and neighboring.

But I guess we were all obtuse about the music for a party we gave for our visiting English friend Norman Storey. We thought it would be interesting if Norman, an antiquarian London bookseller, could have a taste of old-time American country fun, so we invited some of our fiddle-playing, banjo-picking neighbors to come and play for a square dance.

The party was merry and noisy and lasted late, and when it was over and the musicians packed up their instruments we slipped the leader of the group what we considered a very modest fee. Olivia's son, Lloyd Johnson, a rangy, dark-eyed boy who plays the banjo, saw the transaction and was wounded.

"You *paid!*" he said accusingly.

"Well, yes," we admitted. "Some of you came quite a distance, and you certainly gave us a good time."

"You're neighbors," he said, "and you asked us to give a visitor a good time."

We floundered around in apologies and

explanation, but Lloyd was unpacking his banjo.

"I'm going to play you a tune you can't pay for," he said, taking his seat by the hearth.

The last guest had long since departed and was at home in bed, but the family sat spellbound by the fireplace while this dark-haired boy, descendant of mountain troubadours, wove for us on banjo strings a magic compounded of Elizabethan ballads and neighborly caring.

He played us lively buck-dance tunes his grandfather, Lum Crow, using a homemade banjo with a cat-skin head, had taught him. We asked for "Barbary Allen", the old ballad his mother had played on the organ and sung for us so many times before her death, and he search his memory for the words:

"Oh yes I remember in yonder's
    town
In yonder's town a-drinkin'
I give my health to the ladies all
    round
But my heart to Barbary Allen.

"Oh mother, oh mother, go make
my bed,
Go make it long and narr-er,
Sweet William died for me today —
And I'll die for him tomorrow.

"Oh she was buried 'neath the old
church tower
And he was buried a-nigh her
Out of his bosom grew a red, red
rose,
Out of Barbary's grew a greenbrier."

Money is good to have and I don't knock it. But, remembering that night and the young neighbor with the banjo, I am certain that one of the richest gifts you can receive is "a tune you can't pay for."

Gardening

My daughter Mary and my grandson Bird went out to pick the first beans of the season. I had other things to do but I went along to be sure the dew had dried on the leaves before they started. Then I had to pick a few of the pendent emerald pods to be sure that my family knew how to start at the bottom and pick upward, getting the mature beans first.

"Now, Mother, you go on back and do your work," my daughter said. "We know how to pick beans."

Of course they do but the point was that I couldn't stand to see them have all the fun. Harvesting anything in our little postage-stamp garden is a diadem in the crown of plowing, planting, and cultivating. It's an experience to which I look forward for months, maybe the most spirit-lifting, reassuring thing that happens to me all summer.

For seeing a hard, lifeless, pebblelike seed go into the earth and send up a living curtain of rich, dark green leaves which, in turn, offer flowers and then beans is explainable by scientists, I feel sure. But I regard it as pure magic, like unto the feat I saw Blackstone, the magician, perform when I was a child.

It was at the old Lyric Theater in Mobile, and my courtesy cousin Joel (all Southerners have a lot of courtesy cousins and aunts) and I went together. At the height of the performance Blackstone invited all little redheaded girls with a tooth missing to come up on stage and — this was the clincher — bring a little boy with them if they chose. I had red hair and a loose tooth, which Joel promptly yanked out of my mouth, making us both eligible to go forward.

Mr. Blackstone bade us take a newspaper and tear off a piece the size of a rabbit we would like to have. There seems to have been a lot of redheaded, snaggle-toothed little girls in Mobile that summer because we made quite a company on the stage and we must have torn up the complete Sunday edition of the New Orleans *Times-Picayune* into rabbit-sized pieces.

Mr. Blackstone threw these into his top hat, whisked a silk scarf over it, and began pulling out rabbits, a dozen or more rabbits of all sizes. When I think about it I am still mesmerized by the wonder, the pure mystifying magic, of it.

Joel told me it was a trick, unreal. But all I needed to know was that the rabbit I took home was the size of the scrap of newspaper I had torn and real, so real that he promptly ate up all the lettuce in my mother's garden.

The only unreal part of it was that we didn't see how it was done. The same is true of gardening.

A seed is no more impressive than a scrap of paper. The quiet, still earth at a glance is no more dynamic and accomplishing than a black hat. But the mystery is there, the wonder unfailing.

Every time I put seed and earth together and pull out a marigold or a bean I feel just like Blackstone — more gifted, really, because I have reached the time of life when marigolds and beans are far more desirable than rabbits.

Gardening has been a lifelong delight to me — and I certainly don't claim any expertise. My harvests of vegetables are often small and unreliable, my flowers and lawn are scraggly and dejected. House plants sicken and die for me as for the most indifferent beginner. But happily, in gardening as with many things in life, one doesn't have to know a lot or achieve much to have a good time.

My mother played the piano most of her life, not well but enthusiastically. She even embezzled enough of the grocery money when I was eight or ten years old to take lessons. She would drop me off at the library to wait for her on most days, but once I selected my books early and wandered down the street to wait for her on the steps of her teacher's studio. Even I could tell that the sounds coming from the piano weren't impressive. Mrs. Ivy, who whammed out hymns on the out-of-tune old upright at Sunday school, was a better musician. My scales sounded almost as good. And yet the study of the piano made my mother very happy. She wouldn't perform for family, much less company, and it was a source of real regret to her that she wasn't good enough to play in our country church when Mrs. Ivy was absent. But many a summer night when we sat on the porch slapping mosquitos, Muv would slip into the darkened living room and play sweetly, if uncertainly, some little schoolgirl waltz, some plaintive ballad of her youth. If she knew we were listening she faltered, but if we said nothing she played on, loving all the sounds she coaxed from the paino, revering the composer who had had the genius to put them together.

She knew she was no Paderewski, but because she had worked even a little in his field she knew enough to value Paderewski's achievement and her pleasure in all music was enlarged. Her piano teacher got her a ticket to hear Paderewski when he was scheduled to give a concert in

Mobile once, and Muv's excitement was so great that even when the concert was canceled she was not cast down. She *almost* heard him, she often said, and *almost* was a wonder in itself.

So it is with gardening. I have seen some of the great gardens in this country and some that are not so great but far, far better than my fondest dream. And because I have yearned over seed catalogues, spent the grocery money for cow manure, wrenched my back shoveling, and sometimes emerged with little to show for it except dirt under my fingernails, my pleasure in all gardens is multiplied a hundredfold.

I crowed with delight in England over tall Elizabethan walls covered with prodigiously blooming pink clematis because I, too, had struggled to grow clematis with far from spectacular results. I cried out with covetousness when I saw beds of yellow tulips, underplanted with blue forget-me-nots, in Germany because I had rejected tulips as capricious, onetime bloomers and had not been able to persuade forget-me-nots to germinate.

The sight and scent of lilacs along a country road in Wales might not fill all travelers with high excitement, but I have been trying for years to coax a lilac to emulate those in the Walt Whitman poem and ''in the dooryard bloom'' with no success whatever. I had to get out of the car and poke an exploratory finger in the ground to see if I could tell why their lilacs grow as tall as trees and mine merely stays alive.

But, on the other hand, when I saw lavender growing wild on dry hills along the Mediterranean I did not insist on picking a sprig or even rush into a gift shop to buy a lavender sachet for my linen shelves. After all, my two plants are doing rather well themselves. The blossoms they furnish me each June have been sufficient to my needs.

Such small triumphs keep a gardener going, trowel and hoe, for life. For, to reiterate, it's not the results but the doing that is the important thing.

Some of the happiest times I know come during the dreary months of January and February when I find a Sunday afternoon in which to mix potting soil and fill seed pans and start the summer flowers. For a few years now I have been the rich owner of a plastic greenhouse. We got the plans from the University of Georgia's agricultural engineering school and laid out a small investment in short galvanized pipe to drive into the ground, long black plastic pipe to fit over it and make arches and a roll of heavy polyethelene to spread over the arches and staple down. The only sizable expenditure was for a glass door, plywood ends, and running water and electric lines from the house. (A hose and an extension cord would have served but we became ambitious.) We have an old fuel-oil heater a neighbor discarded when he put in central heat and a couple of sacks of pine bark spread on the floor to keep our feet relatively dry.

By greenhouse standards this one is no thing of beauty, but when I come home on a winter night and see its domelike shape frosted over and gleaming in the moonlight, it seems as splendid to me as the gigantic pearl it almost resembles. I can't wait to step out of my town-going shoes and swap my coat for the old raincoat by the back door and rush out to see how things are — to savor the smell of damp earth and to search it for a sprig of green which might have sprouted in my absence.

One winter our heating system broke down and everything died. Another winter the door blew open and I lost cherished plants I had been cosseting for years. But these minor disasters are quickly forgotten the minute you get something else growing again.

Sometimes I wonder what people who don't like to garden dream of in those free snatches of time when they are driving or walking somewhere or are wakeful in the night. You can always worry, of course, and I do my share of that, but if you are determined to rein in your mind and occupy it with happy thoughts, what's better than a garden dream? I spend a lot of time dreaming of the thicket I'm going to have between my cabin and the road or the row of blueberries I am going to plant down the hill. I arrange and rearrange in my mind the herbs and small trailing plants along the rock wall by the back door. This is a pleasant, manageable dream because the plants are small and inexpensive, many of them gifts from friends, and the subtle grays and greens of lamb's ears and pennyroyal, of lavender and apple mint, parsley and chives and tansy and sage provide a fragrance and a texture to dreams that you don't get from clothes or cars or jewelry or even travel.

Oh, the joys of gardening have been celebrated in song and story too many centuries for there to be any doubt that it is one of life's loveliest blessings. According to Genesis, God himself planted the first one: "And the Lord God planted a garden eastward in Eden."

Even before Christ, Horace was expressing a yearning which modern man — and this modern woman — continues to share for "a piece of land not so very large, which would contain a garden, and near the house a spring of ever-flowing water, and beyond these a bit of wood."

Flowers

The natural sequel to gardening is, of course, flower arranging. I hesitate to call it that because the very term bespeaks skills and knowledge which I don't possess. You can spend your life trying to perfect the art of turning a leafless branch and two flowers into a perfect composition in the Japanese tradition. These are courses to take and shows to enter and ribbons to vie for. A whole body of language is involved and enough equipment to outfit a lunar expedition.

All of this interests and attracts me some — not enough for me to take time from something else to spend on it.

It's enough to read an occasional book on flower arranging, mooning over the pictures of prize-winning arrangements, or to drop by a flower show when I can and marvel at the handiwork of the experts. But mostly I stumble along putting whatever flowers I can bear to cut into one of the many bowls and bottles I have collected — and Constance Spry herself couldn't have a better time. (She was the mother of English- and American-style flower arranging, wasn't she?) A house needs fresh flowers, and supplying that need is far more fun than dusting and mopping, which it also needs. I can ignore the dust for weeks, but when leaves and blossoms on yesterday's flowers droop or crisp up I move with alacrity to replace them. So far I haven't inspired my family, much less any real flower arrangers, to cry out in wonderment and admiration at my achievements, But that's all right, I love 'em. Putting them together is my therapy.

In a little log cabin (two log cabins, actually, because we moved another one up and connected it by a breezeway to the first) there are not many places to show off flowers. It is dark, for one thing.

People who built log cabins in 1844 couldn't afford glass or to waste heat with open shutters. But I am faithful to the few places where I can put bouquets — the old harvest table where we eat in the kitchen, the parlor organ by the stairs, the little pine trunk we use for a coffee table in front of the sofa and one end of the mantelpiece.

The real flower arrangers recommend that you cut your blossoms in the evening and condition them, chin deep, in cold water overnight. I have done that on occasion when I wanted to take a long-lasting bouquet to somebody, but routinely part of the pleasure in walking over the yard with a cup of coffee at dawn is spotting and cutting something fresh for the table. It doesn't have to be anything grand to please me. One of my favorite "arrangements" — if I can dignify it with that title — is a handful of wild black-eyed Susans and Queen Anne's lace stuffed helter-skelter into the old flat-bottomed copper kettle that once boiled water for tea on an English sailing ship. I love that little kettle and although it has sprung a leak in the years since a friend gave it to me for Christmas, a mayonnaise jar fits handily into it and I use it constantly for summer flowers and in the winter for red-berried greens. Collecting containers is a satisfaction second only to collecting flowers. My great-grandfather's old shaving mug looks sumptuous with roses in it. I brought back from a thrift shop in Berlin a blue-gray enameled cook pot, fat and squatty as any German hausfrau, and it is a charmer when it holds diminutive pink zinnias and sprigs of rosemary or southernwood.

When I aspire to go the Japanese ikebana route I select a piece of driftwood from the untidy assortment we are always hauling back from the beach, bring in three garlic blooms from the garden and arrange them in a tuna-fish can back of an umbel of rhododendron and maybe a hosta leaf or two. The whole thing is set in an old pewter plate with a handful of shells or some rocks to hide the can and the mechanics.

Every time I pass by and see this arrangement against the whitewashed wall of the cabin I take new delight in its component parts — weathered wood, bleached shells, mauve garlic blooms, silver-gray dish. The assembly most certainly wouldn't set any judge's pulses to hammering but to me it is absolutely stunning. And isn't that what art is all about, to fulfill the artist?

Everything I find and bring home from walks in the woods or at the beach shows up eventually either holding flowers or augmenting them. That way my pleasure in each acquisition — shell, rock, piece of wood, or hunk of moss — is doubled. I have a friend who really is a knowledgeable flower arranger, the show and win kind, and I have seen her dazzle an audience with a dahlia or two and some greasy artifact she picked up in an old automobile graveyard. I admire but do not aspire to emulate. Getting rid of junked cars and nasty old pieces of junked cars has occupied too much of my time for me to see beauty in a carburetor or an oil filter.

Less imaginative but useful are the containers to be had at garage and rummage sales. They are usually leftover florist vases from somebody's hospital stay and can be perfectly dreadful — plastic or tortured paper fiber. But on a lucky day you may find something pretty and well proportioned, if not distinguished.

My daughter Susan once got me a boxful of old florist vases at a church bazaar. It was the end of the day and nobody wanted them, so she bought the whole batch for a dollar. In the lot there's a shallow green bowl which looks pretty filled with pansies, a dark green goblet that welcomes daffofils in the spring, a severely plain pottery bowl that enhances almost anything you put in it, and a plump little yellow pottery vase which is charming loaded with marigolds and those wonderfully lasting, woody-stemmed perennial sunflowers, which look like chrysanthemums but are neater. To make this arrangement look bigger and important enough for a place on the kitchen table, I set it on a wooden cheese board and heap red and yellow peppers at its feet.

There are several others I haven't done anything with, including one plastic fake Grecian urn, but I keep them on shelves on the back porch and look at them often, confident that the day will come when they will be indispensable. I always remember that pink pottery sugar bowl I bought at the Salvation Army thrift store for thirty-five cents and how handily it came in one day when I wanted to send my friend Marda a bouquet of pink thistles. Marda's ancestors were Scottish and her parents admired the national flower so much that they gave it to her for a middle name. In the late summer when there is a particularly handsome stand of thistles by the creek down the road I always try to send Marda, a city-dweller, a bouquet. Thistles are very stylish-looking flowers anyhow, and when you set them off with spikes of blue salvia and maybe a handful of the cream-colored lilliput zinnias which volunteer among the squashes, they come out looking rather elegant. And it's always nice to be able to say, "Keep the vase."

With rummage-sale and thrift-store vases

that is easy enough, but there are some not a whit more valuable, that I can't bear to part with. A small red enameled saucepan pleases me when I set it on the Franklin stove on the back porch and fill it with red fantasy zinnias and the white pompomlike blooms from garlic chives. A small rose-painted cream pitcher with only a slight nick in the spout is lovely filled with pale pink sweetheart roses and lavender or rosemary. I am partial to an old hatpin holder, handed down to me by a beloved cousin, who received it for Christmas or a birthday when she was a teen-ager about the turn of the century. Any single blossom and a leaf or two make an arrangement in that. I cherish an old ironstone vegetable dish for the way it accommodates larkspur, poppies, and cornflowers, and I hang on to a copper preserving kettle for its way with chrysanthemums and autumn leaves.

Sometimes I have feared that there is an alarming tendency toward the whimsical among us who enjoy fiddling around with flowers. For that reason I was almost glad that the Goodwill cookie jar, shaped and decorated like a child's drum, fell off the table and broke before I could put a miniature Christmas tree in it for the office party. It would have been just too cute, I reasoned. But then who brought home an old yellow rubber overshoe, found in the woods while she was collecting ferns, and planted it with varigated wandering Jew for the terrace? I am almost glad two bean plants came up in it, making it voluntarily — and not just on-purpose — hooty.

Someday, I tell myself, when I have time, I am going to be serious about flower arranging. I'll learn the rules and speak authoritatively of *shin* and *soe* and *hikae*. But I don't know, I might take up the tuba instead or join the Peace Corps. Being an uninhibited amateur with flowers is too much fun to give up.

Grandchildren

The most boring people in the world, my mother once told me, are grandparents. "Just remember," she advised me when my first grandchild was imminent, "nobody wants to look at pictures of your grandchildren."

"That's the truth," said our friend Julia. "Since so many of my friends have become grandparents it's ruined wakes for me."

A wake among the people on the Gulf of Mexico coast, where I grew up, is a prime social occasion, where seldom-seen relatives and friends gather and, if it's a big funeral, reunion sometimes for days, eating and drinking and having a fine time. I started to sympathize with Julia but, as I might have known, she had found a solution.

"I tell them I can't look at their pictures because I left my good glasses at home," she said.

With such admonitions before me I have been meticulous about not hauling pictures of John, Bird, Sibley, Ted, and Susy about and pressing them on defenseless friends. Sometimes it seems to me that I, alone among grandmothers, am perfectly objective about grandchildren. They are no more charming, no more lovable than their parents ahead of them, I say. And then again. . . .

There's something about the perspective, I guess. You have the little distance which allows you to see them better, and some of the things which seemed crucial and of earth-shaking importance when you were rearing your children have had the chaff sifted out of them by the years and you recognize that they are of minor, even trivial, size.

Do I worry about clean hands and faces any more? Not often and not for long. Does a report that one of the little boys has a stunning vocabulary of four-letter words send me screaming for the preacher, the psychiatrist, the expert on criminal psychology? Certainly not. I suggest the big dictionary as a source for more precise and euphonious words, and sometimes they even look into it. The sight of blood isn't nearly so frightening as it once was.

My status among my friends and neighbors no longer depends, if it ever did, on the state of my clothesline or the manner and grooming of children. If their blue jeans are scruffy (and they are) and they forget to stand up when their elders enter the room and say "Ma'am" and "Sir" (and they do), I am not undone. There are, I suddenly realize, more important things in life.

Rules about meals and bedding, which I once regarded as fixed and immutable, have turned flexible. If they want to stay up and read or poke around the yard trying to look at the moon through the telescope, I realize there will be other nights to catch up on sleep.

With these extraneous matters out of the way I am free to embark on one of the happier adventures life holds for any of us — loving and being loved by grandchildren.

Oh, there will be times when the old standards rear their heads. When my eldest granddaughter, Sibley (called Tib), was five I got in a swivet about her underpants. She was then the only girl in the family and I didn't want to see her abroad in the land wearing underpants which were gray except where they were streaked with vivid burnt orange from the clay pile in the front yard or black from something she sat on at the woodpile.

A little girl, I proclaimed to my daughters, should wear snowy white drawers. What happened, they wanted to know, to my long-time aversion to television controversies over soap powder, detergent, bleach, fabric softener? Hadn't I spent a great portion of my life avoiding those heart-to-heart talks about The Better detergents, enzyme presoak versus bottled bleaches?

Yes, I said, but Tib was special. Tib deserved spanky white britches and I was determined to see that she had them. It took me the better part of the day to hit upon a method for whitening Tib's lingerie.

First I tried not one but three enzyme presoak solutions. Then I shoveled in two different kinds of detergent. Then I finished off with a highly recommended bottle bleach. Tib's underwear came out of the dryer looking like somebody's old scrub rag. Finally, with the audacity of a Linus Pauling I tried yellow bar soap, bought at Chadwick's old country store up the road, a rub board, and sunshine for drying.

Talk about miracle cleaning, you never saw whiter drawers. I thought any day television would be seeking me out to go on as a poor woman's Bess Myerson. I even wondered fleetingly who was being considered for the next Pulitzer Prize for scientific discovery.

But these flyers into practical matters are for mothers, not grandmothers. There are so many interesting, arresting things about children it's wasteful to expend time and thought on underpants. If you are lucky enough to have this second time around with children, the word is enjoy, enjoy.

Five or six years ago there was a letter to "Dear Abby" from a woman who complained that her mother-in-law repeats herself. Sometimes, she wrote, this crashing old bore told a story that she had already told twenty times before.

Abby, as usual, served up sensible, humane advice, pointing out that the mother-in-law is probably twenty-five years or more older than her son's wife and that when the daughter-in-law reaches that age herself she might repeat her stories.

It made my heart go out to the mother-in-law, for of course she repeats herself. Who doesn't. Some of us tell our old stories over and over again, not because we have forgotten telling them before but because we like to polish and perfect them or, better still, hear them once more ourselves. Since when, I wondered, do we have to have all fresh, original, and sharp anecdotes and repartee in a family? One of the prime functions of a kind and indulgent family is to serve as an audience. If you can't get your family to sit still for your old chestnuts, you are condemned to a life of silence. It's friends and acquaintances who say, "Yeah, you told me that already."

Relatives, particularly grandchildren, are loving people who won't stop you with a cold reminder that you are being repetitious. They'll round up a fresh audience for you. They'll say, " 'Tine, tell Sally your story about the Christmas orange."

The chances are that Sally hasn't heard it and that makes it awfully nice for everybody. You have the fun of telling your story, your grandchildren, faces alert and attentive, feed you your clue lines, and Sally can't be suffering too much because this is her first time around.

But actually I did sympathize a little with the complaining daughter-in-law because obviously she has no little children to teach her the art of tuning out what she doesn't want to hear. My grandson Bird has brought this skill to a peak of perfection in television watching. He has some goggles which he blanked out with cardboard for wearing when the late, late "creature feature" is too terrifying to watch. He leaves the sound on but he slips the goggles over his eyes to shut out what he doesn't want to see.

The picky daughter-in-law could profit by his example. She'd better anyhow because her day of bucking an unresponsive audience is surely on the way.

Grandchildren are more tolerant of you than their parents are. Maybe it's because they have put up with your foibles for a shorter span of time. Take walking. My grandchildren respond with whoops of pleasure when I propose a walk. In fact, they are often the ones to suggest it. But a couple of years ago at the beach with my daughter Susan, I learned to my dismay that she did not want to take those brisk morning hikes along the water's edge with me. When I shook her awake with what she regarded as the intolerable, before-day energy and enthusiasm of Amanda Wingfield in *The Glass Menagerie*, she told me.

"I hate to walk, Mama," she said. "All

of us hate to walk. We've done it all our lives because you enjoyed it so. But not a one of us likes to walk."

Cut to the quick, I couldn't wait to get home and check with her brother and sister to prove her wrong. Alas, she was right. They explained to me that they have suffered in silence all these years. As her brother put it, "I don't mind walking . . . as far as the car."

The grandchildren, on the other hand, don't merely put up with walking. They propose it and are often the ones who awaken me to get in a nice long "morning walk" before anybody else is up.

It may be that they are indulging me. It may just be, because that is something they learn early. Susy, the baby, was doing it when she was a year old. I taught her to play patty-cake and she did it charmingly, clapping her rosy, dimpled little hands together every time she saw me. Finally I realized that the little pixie with her dark red hair and brown eyes wasn't all that gung-ho about patty-cake herself. She thought I was hooked on the game and she wanted to make me happy.

Now and then somebody raises the boys-versus-girls issue. Young couples deciding ahead of time which sex they prefer for their unborn baby are the worst offenders. You can't go wrong with either, I say.

Little boys sometimes strike me as the most interesting, most appealing people in the world. They have a certain pathos which causes me to choke up at odd and unexpected moments. It's such a tremendous thing to have to grow up and be a man. But, of course, it's a tremendous thing to have to grow up and be a person.

Little boys can do things. They are tinkerers and fixers. They will arrive for a week's visit without toothbrush, pajamas, or a change of clothes but tenderly bearing their favorite fishing rod and reel. They find snakes and kill them and carefully stretch their bodies out in the road to scare you to death when you take that morning walk. They can be wild, screeching Comanches one moment and then the next they will lean gently against you to ask with real concern, "You okay, 'Tine?"

About the time I found myself getting fatuous and doting about boy children our tomboy, Tib, comes romping up with scabs on her knees, mud on her chin, and snarls in her hair and I am caught up once more in the wonder of little girl young'uns.

Having to hold her own with a brother and two boy cousins keeps Tib pretty handy with her fists and her feet. But suddenly she goes all-woman. She puts bath oil in the tub and suffers to scrub her hair and roll it up in curlers. She powders her round, hard little body and asks shyly if she can have perfume to put on her throat and wrists. She goes through the drawer and picks out underwear with lace on it, and thereafter when she moves about it is with a new and very feminine quietness and poise. A sort of lace-next-to-my-skin grace.

At a glance when they come tumbling out of the car into the driveway at Sweet Apple, the four older ones all look alike — a passel of jeaned and sneakered rambunctious young'uns. Tib's hair is only slightly longer than the boys' and her jeans are as disreputable, her T-shirt as saggy. But then you notice that she is bringing in a shoe box containing new patent-leather slippers.

She will play with the boys for a while, but presently she passes through the room, heading for that shoe box. "I'd better try on my shoes," she says, "to see if they still fit."

Then she comes back into the kitchen with a small secret smile lifting the corner of her mouth and she is especially gentle and careful when she picks out the knives and forks and plates to set the table. The hand she extends to lift the head of a drooping daffodil in the centerpiece seems unnaturally clean and there is a soft, maternal note in her voice when she says, "Can we make biscuits for supper? I think the boys would enjoy them."

Boys versus girls?

That "versus" is often part of the fun, I admit. But the real truth is that you can't beat having some of each, particularly if they are grandchildren.

Time

Boredom is such an accepted state in this life hardly anybody recognizes it for the fearful voice it can be. German philosophers knew about it, all right. Nietzsche said, "Against boredom even the gods themselves struggle in vain." And Schopenhauer ranked boredom up there with pain as a "foe of human happiness."

It's inescapable that fear of being bored drives people to restless wandering, looking for distraction and entertainment and excessive acquisition of things. Commerce in our country would probably fold up if we bought only what we need instead of eternally seeking something fresh, new, and different. With the spoiled child in one of Louisa May Alcott's stories

(I think *An Old-Fashioned Girl*) we cry, "Amoose me! I want to be amoosed!"

A gifted but perennially miserable friend of mine knew boredom for the monster it can be. She was always roaming from store to store, buying clothes and more clothes, which she seldom wore, taking planes to distant cities, and then holing up fearfully in a hotel room because she didn't like strangers and she had no curiosity about places.

Once I met her coming in from a shopping expedition and I asked her what she had bought.

"A new dress, for my morale," she said.

"You have the most pampered morale I ever saw," I said jokingly.

But she didn't think it was funny. To my surprise she ducked her head and I thought I saw her mouth tremble. Her hands twisted the bag containing the new dress, and when she looked up I saw the vulnerability in her face.

"You see, I have no inner resources," she said pitifully.

It was such a cliché, inner resources, I

felt she might be offering it satirically. But she wasn't. None of us knew it for sure for a long time, but she suffered from a terrible sickness which later caused her to kill herself.

I don't think it was the pain of existence which did her in but the sterility, the tedium, what she said — the lack of inner resources. With the actor George Sanders, whose suicide note said simply, ''I'm bored,'' she found the dailiness of life insupportable.

Looking back, I am ashamed to say I had little patience with her malady. To complain of being bored was immoral by my mother's standards, as well as tiresome inconvenience to your busy family and friends. With the precious gift of time and things to do, you'd be some kind of dumb ingrate to complain of boredom.

Unfortunately, I cannot with the Pharisee thank God I am not as other men. I have been bored, eye-glazed, mind-numbed, seat-paralyzed bored. I have listened to — and made a few — civic-club speeches. I have covered politicians with one set oration and 159 counties in which to deliver it. I have been to a fair number of cocktail parties in my time, where nobody knows anybody else and, worst of all, nobody really talks to anybody else.

Sure, I have been bored.

But when I have time to think about it I am humbly grateful that it is not a way of life with me. The plague of boredom generally passes me by. The dailiness of my life usually fills me with content, if not always with excitement. James McBride Dabbs, that marvelous old South Carolina teacher and writer, wrote that the pinnacles of heaven "rise all about us, though most of them stand hardly above the grass and may, like fairy castles, be crushed by a careless step." I am sure he did not mean that those pinnacles exist solely in the physical world, although he said of Southerners: "We are the land's to a greater degree than most Americans. We belong to it."

Because I am southern and strongly attracted to the earth and what the Bible calls "the fullness thereof" I owe most of my daily pleasure in living to pinnacles no taller than a blade of grass. I awaken early, unable to stay in bed after dawn because of the pull of the out-of-doors. That is true since I moved to the country, and it was true when I lived in the city with only a postage-stamp-sized yard to plant and work in. But I needed then and I still need to see the day, examine the color of the sky, assess the weather, and, whatever the season, check the progress of a plant, touch the soil.

If I have a day to spend at home in the country I am intoxicated with the possibilities of pleasure — the gardening I can do, the walks or bicycle rides I can take. If the weather rules out these enterprises, staying indoors is far from boring. There's always cooking, which I love, and housecleaning, in which I can take a macabre kind of interest, and if these fail for any reason, there's sewing, knitting, music to listen to, books to read. Because there are so many things I want to do I find myself trying to do too many of them at once, burning the roast and dropping stitches while I try to cook, read, and knit at the same time.

But the real reason I have seldom been bored, I believe, is that I love my job. A newspaper job has more variety, introduces you to more different kinds of people, than any job in the world. You meet knaves and rogues and scoundrels, poets, politicians, and philanthropists, murderers, ministers, and movie stars. You know astonishingly bad people and astonishingly good people, sometimes with these elements well mixed in one person. There's even an occasional bore but of such monumental proportions that even as you listen to his pompous and monotonous maunderings you marvel at the range and scope of his dullness.

More frequently, your day is enhanced by the arrival of a bona fide nut — a lady who has come to help you pray because the world is coming to an end at precisely 4:15 P.M. or a man who is tortured by the voices he hears in the air and thinks you may know the secret incantation which will vanquish them.

It wasn't a typical day but not too atypical, at that, the summer afternoon when I interviewed Lady Nancy Astor and covered a wedding in a meat-packinghouse picket line within moments of each other. (The bridegroom worked in the wiener room, the bride worked in the egg room. They met and were married in the picket line and we all adjourned to the Stockyards Cafe for the wedding reception, at which the juke box played "She's Too Fat for Me.")

Maybe only in a newspaper job are you eternally enriched by the unexpected. A couple of Christmases ago I went to say a few words to open the Salvation Army's Christmas bazaar. There was a young man there who wanted to speak to me, a Salvationist told me before the program started. A nice-looking kid waited for me in a back room. He told me his name and then he said cheerfully, "I'm that garbage-can baby you wrote about twenty years ago. Remember? They found me stuffed in a garbage can covered with ants, and they kept me in the hospital a long time because they thought I was mentally retarded."

"And you're not!" I cried in surprise.

He grinned. "I could have been. But a lady read your story about me to her husband, a blind man, and they decided to take a chance on me. They had a farm and a bunch of children of their own and not a whole lot else besides love. They shared all they had with me — and it turned out that was all I needed."

Somebody touched my shoulder and led me away to do my part in opening the Christmas bazaar and somehow I stumbled through it. But it was a sloppy job. I couldn't see much for the tears in my eyes.

Bored? How can you be when you contemplate the hope and the anguish, the diversity and infinite possibilities of life?

Work

She is an old lady who lives alone down the road a piece, a marvelously spunky, lively woman who by her wit and her accomplishments attracts a constant stream of visitors to the blooming dooryard and the neat litle tarpaper-covered house beyond it. Once I remarked that she was wise, and she laughed aloud.

"The Lor-rd," she said, drawing it out. "How could I be wise? I never had more than a year's schooling if you put it all together. That's not wise, that's ignorant."

I tried to explain that I was talking about wisdom learned not from books but from life. I told her what Emerson said (not quoting him by name, of course, because that would have seemed pretentious) about drudgery, calamity, exasperation, and want being instructors in eloquence and wisdom.

"Only so much do I know, as I have lived," I quoted, and she nodded her head vigorously.

"I know that," she said. "If I hadn't a knowed that, there has been many a thing I couldn't alived through. You face 'em, you make the best of 'em, and you go on."

She shook out her apron and hung it on a peg by the kitchen stove and led the way into the little room where her quilt scraps, her bonnets, and the rag dolls she makes to sell awaited her.

At night and in the heat of the day, when it is too hot to work in her garden or can and freeze vegetables and fruits for her winter larder, she sews. She picked up her work and hunted for her thimble, and then she paused and, tilting her head to one side, grinned puckishly.

"I know a secret," she said, "and I think you know it too."

"I do?" I said. "What?"

She whispered the word: "Work."

"That's the secret?" I asked.

"It's the secret," she said solemnly. "Folks are in a quarrel about work now. A lot of them think it's a burden and a blight. If they could be shed of it they think they'd be happy. Young ones think it's a sin, a sign that the old ones is greedy and covetous, wanting the wrong things like too much money. We know better, don't we?"

"Well, I *like* to work," I said defensively.

There have been times when I've wondered if that were the sign of a weak character, a poverty of imagination, or mental illness. When I first read F. Scott Fitzgerald I began to wonder guiltily if I shouldn't have something better to do than work. When the flower children of San Francisco gave up gainful employment to sit in the sunshine and talk up love and peace I thought maybe they, like Mary, sister of that pushy housewife Martha, in the Bible, had not chosen "the better part."

A handsome bearded young fellow I

know who traveled over the country in a trim, precisely outfitted old pickup truck, sleeping under trees, and sometimes pitching camp in a borrowed barn to fish a few days and rest and read, told me nine-to-five work was a crutch to save the weak and the fearful from gibbering collapse. If he needed money for food, he worked a few days in a field or a factory. When winter came, if he needed shoes (he went barefoot all summer) or a part for his truck, he did the same. To want more, he suggested, a stable home, a better car, hospital insurance, and a retirement plan, was a sign of middle-class weakness. To choose work as a way of life was to choose bondage, involuntary servitude, he said.

"You want to travel, you want to see the world," he said, waving his hand expansively. "Go, see!"

I'm always insecure about talking to the young, and I saw a bee bobbing on a begonia blossom and cravenly latched on to it as an excuse.

"I'd want a place to come home to," I mumbled desperately. "My bees . . . my bees would hate to travel."

The young man smiled patronizingly into his splendid black beard and said something about the corrupting influence of possessions and borrowed some tools and left.

And even as I watched him go I knew I hadn't told the truth. I love to work.

I wouldn't mind sleeping under a tree or giving up hospital insurance (I'm practically never sick), but I'd feel lonely and displaced and useless without a job.

As a child of the Depression I grew up with a perhaps unnatural respect for work. I saw men in breadlines and flophouses, and hunger and deprivation weren't what was breaking their hearts and corroding their spirits. It was the feeling of being totally useless, unneeded, unwanted. To have work to do, work that you believe in and value, is one of the greatest blessings a human being can claim.

I got my first newspaper job when I was fifteen years old, and except for time out to get a little schooling and later to have three babies, I have been at it steadily ever since. I have been tired and disgusted, sometimes disillusioned. Once in a fit of pique I walked off my job, vowing to find more congenial work washing dishes or mopping floors somewhere. Fortunately, to my enormous relief, my boss and I straightened out our differences and I never got so far as cleaning off my desk. It would have been a terrible wrench. Not that I'd mind dishwashing or mopping all that much, but I'd miss the sights and sounds, the smells and the pressures and the high purpose of a newspaper office. For, despite its weaknesses and misses and near misses, newspapering is dedicated to something important — letting the people know.

To have been a part of that endeavor has made me proud through the years, but pride isn't enough to sustain you when you have personal problems and hurts. Even pride in the knowledge that you can earn a living of sorts for your family grows old and a little saggy when other things in your life are out of kilter. But the work itself is a great palliative. Blows which would have felled me if I had had time to stay home and dampen a pillow with my tears have always shifted into focus when I have had to go to work and hold them up against other people's problems. Courts and jails and hospitals, fires and floods and flophouses are a newspaper reporter's hunting ground, and in them you see real, raw pain and sometimes real, raw courage. It shames and humbles you and, in some perverse way, it pushes you toward a better handling of your portion of adversity.

There are things in all our lives to rob us of joy and spirit and strength. I have gone to work sometimes feeling utterly drained, incapable of holding up my head and putting one foot ahead of another because of pain or loss, which I thought had flattened me. But as I approached the building — and it's been true of all the buildings in which I have worked in thirty years — I have felt a subtle lifting of my spirits, a budding excitement. When I have walked into the newsroom with its familiar noise and disorder, its throb and push, and its dear, screwball people, I have never failed to have a sense of homecoming. I have told myself that my knowledge and my skills will never be great enough for the task, my inspiration will never be vibrant enough, nor the hours I put in long enough. But such competence as I possess has been rewarded here. In a sometimes hostile world I have found refuge here; when I felt rejected elsewhere I was among friends here.

Sometimes I think of the day when the city editor sent me out to get a story on a young man, an Emory law student, who had been struck down and instantly killed by a hit-and-run driver as he crossed the street on his way home on a rainy night. It was just another story, and I didn't think much about it until I arrived at the home of the young man's mother.

She was a woman I knew at church, and she thought I had come to pay a sympathy call. She put her arms around me and cried, and then she drew up her pregnant young daughter-in-law and her grandchild for me to meet. They were all in a state of shock and their grief was so fresh and poignant I thought I couldn't bear it. But I had to introduce a photographer and get out pencil and paper and write down names and ages and asked them to lend me their own picture of the dead boy. It seemed to me then that setting briskly about my business of getting a story for the paper was the most callous, unfeeling intrusion I had ever seen, and I felt so shaken by the experience that I couldn't face the newsroom or the man who had sent me on the assignment. I trailed the photographer back to the studio and slumped on a desk there, tired and angry and resentful.

"I hate this job!" I cried to Kenneth Rogers, longtime head of our photographic department. "I hate poking about in other people's tragedies!"

My old chums in photo couldn't understand my sudden disaffection for a business they knew I loved, my revulsion at a story which in the scope and range of the day's news didn't loom very big or very important. One man, a rainy night, a car . . . a little family. . . . People had been dying by the thousands in the war just ended; what was I so upset about?

"But I *knew* these people!" I cried. "They thought I had come out of *sympathy!*"

If the photographers thought my feelings were excessive they didn't say so. They let me sit there on the desk and cry and then they dried me off and sent me downstairs to write. Sensitivity to the pain of others was important, Kenneth told me as he walked me to the elevator. Maybe I would write a better story.

Well, I'm sure it wasn't much of a story. I haven't read it in years. It came out on page one — a simple "Memo to a Hit-and-Run Driver," telling him what he had done, showing him a picture of the young girl so cruelly widowed and the little boy and the mother. As far as I could make it, it was a straightforward recital of the facts, devoid of feeling.

The next day an alcoholic read it in a bar and called me on the phone. He had a foggy notion that he had hit something or someone that night in the rain. What should he do? I told him to call the police, and he did. A dent in his fender and blood and hair matching those of the young victim would have been enough to convict him anyhow, but he chose to plead guilty.

Even believing that justice had prevailed, I couldn't be happy about that story. The hit-and-run driver was a sick alcoholic but otherwise a good man — and he, too, had a wife and children who loved him.

The little story won an Associated Press award that year. I couldn't help wishing it had been for something else.

Very few stories win prizes, of course, and even more important, you can't always count on them to produce results — the surrender of a wrongdoer, the cleanup of corruption, the fireproofing of a nursing home or a mental institution. You can't count on it, but it happens often enough to affirm your belief in the magic of the words *"Let the people know,"* and to convince you that you are fortunate to have a hand in that process.

Not all work is like that, I know. Studs Terkel's bestselling book *Working* dramatically points up the drudgery that is a way of life for many people, the sense of entrapment thousands feel as they go to their jobs.

Sometimes I wonder if I am not a bit

like the feeble-minded girl Onie in Margaret Long's fine book *Louisville Saturday:*

> Then Onie, flushed once more with success, put the bucket on the floor. . . . Now she bent over eagerly, to dip the mop in the sudsy water and dunk it up and down, enjoying the rite of the slurp-slurp. Then, rather triumphantly, she drew out the mop and slapped it on the linoleum, watching the suds and bubbles slide and twinkle across the floor in its wake. She pushed the mop back and forth, back and forth, smiling as the clear, clean streaks and swirls shone brightly through the dirt as she worked. . . . Her happiness bubbled inside her like a spring freshet as she opened the window and emptied out the bucket of dark water. . . .

Retarded or not, those of us who have work we love and love to work, as my old neighbor down the road suggests, have a hold on at least one of contentment's secrets.

Land

"Before you die you must own a bit of land — maybe with a house on it that your child or your children may inherit. . . ."

The speaker is the old mother in Betty Smith's *A Tree Grows in Brooklyn*. She is talking to her daughter, Katie, following the birth of Katie's first child, Francie. But she speaks for all of us whose ancestors came to this country from the Old World, where they owned nothing, except the right to live and work on some other man's land.

Following her mother's advice, Katie nailed a condensed-milk can to the darkest corner of the closet floor of every tenement in which the family lived and put five cents in it every day even if it meant going hungry or cold. At the last when Johnny, the charming alcoholic father, died, they had to spend the little money that had accumulated in the can to buy him a grave — and Katie never nailed the milk can to the closet floor again.

"We won't need it any more," she told her children, putting the deed to the cemetery lot on top of the clumsy star-shaped bank, where it sat on the kitchen table. "You see, we own a bit of land now."

The desire to own land became an unholy passion with some immigrants. I remember a family story of a man from Sweden who starved and overworked his wife and children, always with the determination to buy land, more land, all the land that adjoined his. In that time, of course, ownership of land constituted class distinction. A property owner was the lovely English-sounding thing — a freeholder, therefore entitled to serve on juries and participate in bond elections. A new kind of snobbery was born.

Once my mother gave me an example of

our ancestors' feeling on the subject. We were looking at a little glass cream pitcher which had belonged to her grandmother Susan Hinson.

Muv was partly reared by her grandmother and admired and loved her very much.

"Poor Grandma," she said, turning the little pitcher in the light. "She bought this at Henry Paulk's store in Willacoochee before she married Grandpa. I guess you could say it is an antique now because they were married long before the Civil War."

I asked how she knew about that particular piece of glass when she wasn't certain of the origin and age of so many of her grandmother's things. She knew because the pitcher was a family symbol of independence, of faith, and of love.

Grandma, Muv explained, had, in the classic southern phrase, been "raised nice," which is to say she had Advantages — a melodeon in the parlor and education at a Female Academy. Her parents were big landowners, and they had every intention of making their daughter Susan a lady. But Susan fell in love with a renter — a poor man who had no land of his own! That was hard for her parents to take, and they tried to nip the romance in the bud — with no success. Determined, young Susan wanted to start accumulating a trousseau and house fixings for her coming marriage. Her parents, so indulgent in other ways, would give her no help, offer her no money. Finally with a bit of pocket money she happened to have she bought the only thing she could afford — the little cream pitcher — and ran off and married her renter.

It turned out that Great-grandpa had no intention of being that hated thing, a renter, long. He gradually acquired a sizable farm, and I imagine he bought Great-grandma many sets of dishes in time. He had to. They had fifteen children.

The desire to own the roof over your head is strong in most of us, I suppose, but when with the help of borrowed money I "paid down" on my first house it was the ownership of the hard, city-sour backyard which really moved me. The house was an old frame dwelling on a close-to-town street and I loved it and was glad to have the shelter of its sturdy black roof, its thick white clapboard walls. There was room for all of us and some to rent out, and I felt, after some years of roaming, that I had a fixed and secure place in the world for the first time since I had grown up and left my parents' house.

The afternoon we moved in our few possessions — a big walnut desk, some boxes of books and dishes, and a borrowed bed — I walked out in the backyard and looked at the sweetgum tree. It was an enormous tree, its girth so great it would have taken two long-armed men to reach around it, its branches towering above the two-story roof.

It stood squarely in the center of the backyard, and although I was to learn later that its roots grabbed off all the nourishment in the hard-packed earth and its branches appropriated the sunshine, at that moment it was to me the prettiest thing on earth. My tree, my own tree.

My husband was recovering from a minor heart attack and had gone to bed and to sleep as soon as we could set up the bedstead with its mattress and springs. But I was caught up in the excitement of the move, the unbelievable accomplishment of having bought a house — *land!* — and I wandered around the premises, restless most of the night.

The children had been staying with Muv in Florida, waiting for me to find a place, and now they would be arriving very soon. The weeds were tall in the yard. The grass had not been cut in months. The house needed cleaning, needed curtains and furniture, a stove, a refrigerator — things we would be a long time acquiring. But in the meantime we had a tree — and *land*.

I spread a pallet on the floor of the little screened porch off the bedroom, where I could see the branches of my tree, with its star-shaped leaves against the sky, and spent the rest of the night looking at it and listening to the wind stirring around in it.

The tree was my friend as no borrowed tree could ever be. Through all the seasons of the next seventeen years that tree was the last thing I saw as I dropped off the sleep at night, the first thing I saw on awakening in the morning. I loved it both in full leaf and bare-branched, but I loved it with a passion in the spring when its sticky, pale gold buds first told me winter had ended and in the fall when it became a living bonfire of rich and joyful color. There were other, smaller trees in the backyard and one spectacular red oak in the front yard, but the sweetgum was *my* tree, signifying my ownership of the land which nurtured it and us. For although we couldn't grow anything much in that shady city soil, least of all food crops, the children and I always felt stronger and had some sense of status in a mostly precarious world because we, in the hackneyed phrase, "owned our own home." We didn't move around like the apartment-dwellers who went off owing my son a week's paper bill. We were known to the corner druggist and the grocer and especially the postman. He was a black man named Mr. Clinton Davis, who always suffered with us over bad news and rejoiced with us when there was good news. He knew when the children were away and that in my anxiety to hear from them I would be hanging around in the front yard waiting for the mail before I would go to work.

To relieve my suspense he would start waving the moment he turned the corner and started down the hill.

"Card from Jimmy today!" he would call out. Or, "The girls got to camp safely, I see. You heard from them today!"

Ownership of that city lot and the old house on it, ownership of that tree, symbolized for us permanence in a shifting, changing world. We were citizens who could complain to the mayor if we wanted to and complain with authority because weren't we also proud taxpayers?

When I sold the house in town to move to the country I saw them begin to raze the building to make way for an apartment complex, and I stayed away after that, fearful that I might chance by just as they began to saw down my tree. It was bad enough to see the walls which had sheltered us totter and fall, but I couldn't have stood the whine of the saw and the near-human scream of the tree as it fell.

The ownership of a bit of land with a log cabin on it in the country was an adventure, but it lacked the impact of a *first*. I had already owned land, signed papers, had a mortgage and a deed, and I thought the blush had gone from the experience. And then I stood in the driveway which we had hacked from a tangle of wild plums, honeysuckle vines, and blackberry briers and looked at the sun on the walls of the little cabin. I felt like the pioneer woman who must have seen them rise that day in 1844. It was dilapidated; many people said it was impractical and would be worse — uncomfortable — but I felt a kinship with it, a deep and abiding satisfaction with it.

Restoring it took more time and money than I dreamed it would, and people were almost right about comfort. When the wind blows through the cracks between the logs in winter and the electricity goes off and the pipes freeze, it can be very uncomfortable. But then we build fires in the big rock fireplaces and set a kettle on the coals to heat and draw the curtains and pull up our rocking chairs, and it seems to me that is the most comfortable place in the world.

There's a sense of continuity about living in your own place. It's your land and, barring subdivisions, death, and other disasters, you both are going to be there. You fall into step with the rhythm of the seasons, making a pact with the maple tree by the well house and the climbing rose by the corncrib to see each other through.

Muv

We have seen death in our family. My father died and then my children's father. We lost two babies very tragically. We have lost friends we thought we could not live without.

Then we lost Muv.

One morning in June she called and said she had another pain in her chest — this one worse than the first one six weeks earlier. I was on my way, I told her, but she was to let a friend who was there standing by take her to the hospital immediately.

"I might and I might not," said Muv.

"Go on," I urged. "I'll be there as fast as I can get there."

"I don't want that," she said. "I just

wanted you to know."

Six hours later, when my son and I drove up to her gate, we found the yard and porch full of neighbors. Muv, they said, had died in her sleep about an hour before.

It seemed to me then and for days afterward that the death of my mother was a loss I could not accept. The mind knows the cold biological facts. The valiant old heart was still, the weary body had been taken away to be prepared for burial in the ragged, sun-baked little graveyard where other members of her family were already. But I kept hearing Muv's voice in the house, expecting to see her on the narrow spool bed where she had slept since the death of my father. When a friend who had been sitting with the group of callers on the porch stood up to go in the house, I put out a hand and touched her arm. "See about Muv," I whispered before I thought.

I found myself holding things to tell her or to show her — the notes that came, the newspaper stories about her death, the things people said. The habit of expecting her interest had been so strong on me all my life, how could I give it up at once? As a child she had let me tell her the plots of stories I read or movies I saw. When I was a teen-ager she had listened with what I took to be absolute absorption to my accounts of the happenings at school or in my first newspaper job. Later when I was facing the problems and pleasures of love and marriage and child-rearing, she was always ready to hear me and to help me if she could. She who had been indestructibly *interested* in whatever life had to offer — how could I believe that death had detached her and shut away that bright attention?

Once years ago when my problems had seemed too painful and too complex to handle Muv and I had sat up late discussing them. Finally she had sighed resignedly and laughingly summed up.

"And, honey," she said, "we can't expect to escape by dying, because the women in our family live forever!"

She had fooled me, I thought. She had not lived forever.

Oh, I knew what her minister would

say. He had spoken to me as if she were taking a trip to a fairer land. And that was all right. I could believe that, not knowing exactly where that land is or what it's like. But I wasn't reconciled. I wanted her where I could reach her, where I could talk to her. I wanted her laughter, her scorn, her outrageous jokes and satire. Having her live in glory, as they said, was small comfort to me. What did Muv, who thought Paris, France, looked like Dothan, Alabama, know about glory?

One of the specialties in death's bag of tricks is that it sharpens recollection and, oddly enough, the memories it leaves are the good ones. Muv herself pointed that out to me, and I thought of it again when we went back after the funeral to look at the little mound of earth under its blanket of white flowers. In the row of her relatives' graves was the tombstone of a reckless, colorful young fellow who had married one of her cousins. One morning several years ago when I had troubles I thought were at least vaguely disgraceful, Muv and I took a walk to discuss them and we went by the cemetery.

"You see that stone," Muv said, pointing to the young man's grave. "He was married to our cousin and they weren't happy and she tried to leave him. One day he took a gun and said he was going to kill her and then himself. She had a gun and she shot first. He died a few days later, after telling everybody it was his own fault, but we thought at the time that we would never live down the disgrace."

Muv reached out and rubbed a finger over the name carved in marble.

"Now who remembers? Who cares? Death cuts away the error, and those who remember him at all remember that he was handsome — and *spirited.*"

Muv herself was spirited, and I remember that rather than the final weeks of her life when she was in pain and sometimes limp and querulous. We tell and retell our stories about her and I think we are through with tears but not with laughter.

I thought I knew about death and grief but I don't really. I only know that you learn one small thing at a time. I came eventually to regard my mother's death as a blessing because she was old and we could foresee certain suffering and weakness and possible invalidhood for her. How could my strong, self-reliant mother accept dependency and helplessness? She would loathe it. The thought of leaving her own house and living where she could be "looked after" infuriated her. She was in control of her life as long as possible, and when it was no longer possible she went to her bare little room with its narrow bed and lay down and died. I feel now that it was her choice, that she willed herself to have done with life. That she pulled it off seems to me to be both her personal triumph and a blessing.

But there is another blessing, and that is that she will live, if not forever, at least as long as her family and friends are alive and remember.